Finding Myself...Facing Cancer

By Sarah Fenlon Falk

Dedications

To my parents, Gary and Susan Fenlon,
for always believing

For Pete, Bobby, Teddy, Sam, and Will:
You are My Loves and My Life

And to the always-generous Cindy Heimberger,
who gave me the gift of this title

Book Project Contributors

While there were many who participated in this cancer journey in significant ways whether through financial contributions, by caring for my family and me during my cancer treatment, with meals or with a shoulder to cry on, these pages are dedicated to those who specifically gave to my family and I in some way so that the idea of this book would become a reality. If you are among those who played a role in supporting this project and supporting me through this cancer experience: your part in my life is irreplaceable.

Cheryl and Dave Palmer in memory of Barbara Palmer
Susan and Doug Palmer in memory of Barbara Palmer
Susan and Gary (Mom and Dad) Fenlon
Doralee and Merrill (Mom and Dad) Falk
Cindy Heimberger
All Anonymous Donors
Manteno United Methodist Church, Manteno, Illinois
River of Life Church, Cheboygan, Michigan
Kankakee Area Senior Providers Group
Keystone Counseling, Bourbonnais, Illinois
Herscher School District, Herscher, Illinois
Presence Home Care, Bourbonnais, Illinois
The Cancer Support Center of Homewood and Mokena, Illinois
Julia and Corey Moles

Waves of Grace

NBC 5 Chicago and Lexus Salute to Survivors

Brushes With Cancer, a Twist Out Cancer event

Kelli Bonomo, Nutrition 360

Jonathan Rand, Enlightened Entrepreneur and Writer's Guide

Mary Harris, Editor Extraordinaire and sister in cancer-survivorship

Kristen Martin and Vivien Reis, for their YouTube series on writing and self-publishing

Thank you, all!

Introduction

Written in 1992 during treatment for bone cancer:

There's no easy way around it—cancer eats away at not only the physical, but also the emotional and spiritual parts of a person as well. It's been eating me up for months. I've felt the urge to write, scream, or say *something* against my invisible foe...but the words won't come out, and what good would a scream do? I've wanted all along to write something that will not only help me to get through this tough time, but something that also may be useful to others going through the same trials.

I pray that what I write will not be my words alone, but would be God's words of comfort and courage to all who are hurting and seeking. An answer to those who ask the question, "Why?" for those with, or without, cancer.

Written in 2015 during treatment for breast cancer:

Cancer as a seventeen-year-old teenager and then again as a forty-one-year-old wife and mother holds stark contrasts when the experiences are put up against one another, but do hold some similarities as well. I will be sharing from my journals as a seventeen- and eighteen-year-old, as well as thoughts and journal entries from my forty-one-year-old self.

—

You, dear Reader, will read about the impact this experience has had on me: emotionally, physically and spiritually. The effects of this diagnosis upon my husband Pete and our four boys are also discussed. I do hope all that I share will serve to comfort, encourage, and inspire you. And that these things I have written will give insight into the life of a cancer patient, survivor or caregiver in a way that will uplift those who need it.

2/10/15
The Night Before

So, here it is. The night before...or at least it was when I started writing. I always have trouble sleeping the night before: the night before the first day on the job, the night before the big game, the night before vacation. Imagination stirs the night before Christmas, the night before the important interview, and/or the night before the test.

That's the one. For me tonight, it's the night before the test, exam, procedure. I'll be having a breast biopsy in twelve hours and I can't sleep. There have been so many thoughts and emotions swirling around inside of me for the last week or two that I can't even see straight. I'm not sure what to think or feel. I'm having trouble getting to sleep. I need to lay it all out here.

In July of 1991, I was in the same situation. The night before the biopsy of my left femur at the Mayo Clinic in Rochester, Minnesota is a night I'm not likely to ever forget. We hadn't called ahead for reservations so we found a little hotel room (or was it a motel?) just outside of Rochester. My parents and I were crammed into a tiny room with a king bed. The front desk personnel hauled in a cot for me, (which at just 5'3" I was still too long for!) and my mom made it up for me. This was not acceptable to me and I pitched a good fit about it.

That night, showering before bed, something snapped or broke in me. I wept, or wailed, or sobbed. It came from the very depths of me and poured out of my eyes and was vocalized through my cries. I was grieving and I could feel it at the very core of my being. I've never felt anything quite like it before or since. It was as though my spirit, my very soul knew the blow I would be dealt the following day and the difficult journey I was about to embark upon.

When I finally emerged from the bathroom, my mother was crying too. She and my father prayed over me, spoke to me, and comforted me as only loving parents can do and I did not sleep on the cot that night.

Now, with all this cancer talk: I want to be clear that I haven't been diagnosed with anything at this point. The procedure that I will have tomorrow, February 11, 2015, will identify the lump/mass/ calcification that was discovered just over a month ago. But as I'm facing a biopsy and "possible" diagnosis, it's no wonder that I'm reflecting on a *previous* biopsy and its results.

My world today, in 2015, is quite different. I'm no longer a teenager, no longer in school. I am married to a loving and generous man, and I have my four little boys who I miraculously birthed over the last five years. Those boys are miracles because most of my chemotherapy drugs reported infertility as a side effect. Praise God for His grace and gifts! Not only do I have a family of my own these days but I also have what I consider to be a successful career. I work away from home part-time, which has afforded me the blessing of more time with my children. (Time at home can be more stressful than being at the office or out visiting patients, but in the same respect, that is time I wouldn't trade for anything!) My office is the place where I see clients for counseling. I enjoy my private practice and am passionate about the work I do there.

My "day job" is working for a home care agency as a medical social worker. I don't work for just any home care agency, but for a member of the national Home Care Elite. That means we are among the top 25% home care agencies in the whole US of A. It is important work I do there, and I have a great team to work with. I am quite thankful for my employment opportunities.

Also, it was actually just a year ago now, in 2014, that my mom was diagnosed with breast cancer and I wrote my "POV" post on my Mediterranean Experiment blog (which has now been merged with the blog at sarahfenlonfalk.com) to express how I was feeling at the time. Let me just say *that* has been quite a journey in and of itself this last year. This journey was made especially interesting since she chose to follow a holistic regimen rather than seek conventional treatment. She's been doing very well and her cancer count is *way* down. And now it is I going through the process of trying to get some answers for myself with two unidentified lumps to be biopsied tomorrow. I've been struggling with this so far since the last time I had a biopsy it was cancer...that doesn't inspire confidence.

My friend Kristi was praying with me earlier this week about all of this and she used the phrase "girls grown tall" when stressing during her prayer just how much we need our heavenly Father in and for everything. A vision of myself as a little girl with long hair and wearing a sundress was stuck in my mind. I could see myself hugging our Father around the waist and looking up into His face, which was as bright and warming as the sun. In the same instant, I saw myself, as I am now, with all the weight of responsibility and knowledge, just as needy and vulnerable as my six-year-old self. As I contemplated that image throughout the day, I wrote a poem that I've shared on Facebook and will share here as well. I could see my child self *and* my adult self, doing all of the things mentioned in the poem. Ultimately, what I realized was that to our heavenly Father I am *always* a little girl in need of His guidance and care—things He readily and steadily provides. It was a very reassuring and comforting epiphany for me. Funny that the realization of how vulnerable I am led to feelings of peace. But it's only because of the awareness of our Father's constant presence, caring, and provision that there is comfort and peace.

Little Girls Grown Tall

We twirl and play, dance and sing, dream of a wedding and engagement ring.
We are just little girls grown tall after all.
When we want to be heard, we yell and shout, trying to get hard feelings out.
We are just little girls grown tall after all.
We cry out loud, throw ourselves on the bed, look for a strong shoulder on which to rest our head.
We are just little girls grown tall after all.
We stomp our feet when we want our way, for others to listen to what we say.
We are just little girls grown tall after all.
And when we've completed a job well done, we hope to receive a bit of praise, not much—but some.
We are just little girls grown tall after all.
And when we're afraid or feeling so small, we draw close to our Father who to us is so tall.
We wrap our arms around His waist; turn our eyes to look up at His face.
"Father, please help me," is all we can say, in our most helpless, vulnerable, little girl way.
His presence alone calms the nerviest nerve, and His embrace overwhelms with love undeserved.
"My precious child," He says so gently,
"I am always with you, I hear your every call.
"For you are my little girl, just grown tall after all."

—

I wanted to write these things down for myself, for my own encouragement and remembrance, but also in hopes that they might encourage others.

During my cancer experience in 1991-92, my theme Bible verse was Jeremiah 29:11, "'For I know the plans I have for you,' declares the Lord. 'Plans to prosper you and not to harm you. Plans for hope and a future.'"

At this point in my journey, with all that I am facing at this moment and whatever the future may hold, the promise of His presence is now my theme.

"...for He Himself said, 'I will never leave you, I will never forsake you.'" Hebrews 13:5. That amazing promise is on my heart and mind this "night before" and it is what I hold onto. Now, for some sleep...

2/11/15
Let It Be

Let it be. Those were the first words I heard in my head after hanging up with the doctor today. "I just spoke with the pathologist and it's not good news," he had said. And so it was that I was told this afternoon at about 1:31 p.m. that I have breast cancer.

I've been singing the Beatles song in my head since then. With the phrase and the song running through my mind, I decided it might be interesting to look up the story behind the song. Apparently, Paul McCartney was going through an anxious time in his life. One night, he had a dream in which his mother, Mary, appeared to him to help calm him. She had died ten years earlier of cancer. "Let it be" were her words of comfort.

"Let it be," in the first half of the song, means to relax, let go, don't worry about your troubles, accept the bad things that happen.

I'm still in shock and not so sure I can simply relax right now. I know there is much more information that needs to be gathered. We don't know the type or the stage of the cancer. We hope to learn more very soon so we can begin to make decisions for care and treatment.

Even after reading the story behind the Beatles song, I still wondered why I had the phrase "let it be" on my mind. I tried to think of anywhere else I may have heard that phrase and came up with the following scripture: The angel answered and said to her, 'The Holy Spirit will come upon you, and the power of the Most High will overshadow you; and for that reason the holy Child shall be called the Son of God. And behold, even your relative Elizabeth has also conceived a son in her old age; and she who was called barren is now in her sixth month. For nothing will be impossible with God.' And Mary said, 'Behold, I am the servant of the Lord; let it be done to me according to your word.' And the angel departed from her." Luke 1:35-38 (NASB)

Mary, in faith, declared to the angel Gabriel, "Let it be done to me according to your word." She was a willing servant of God. Bearing another baby boy would be a welcome and joyous task compared to what lies before me. But when I look at this verse again and consider it for myself, it was not, "Let it be" that stood out like a neon sign, it was the phrase, "For *nothing* will be impossible with God."

That was what I needed to hear. Yes, "let it be." Remain calm. Don't be anxious. But even more so, at this moment, "Nothing will be impossible with God." I keep reminding myself of this truth as I consider my four small children, my husband, my house, my two jobs... It all seems overwhelming as-is, but to add cancer to that mix feels "impossible." Yet I know that with God all things are possible. I will rest in that tonight.

2/15/15
Weak and Strong in the Deep End

My husband Pete and I were talking in the car on our way to see the surgeon on Thursday afternoon. We were going over the questions we wanted to ask, what (little) we already knew about breast cancer in general, and etc.

"I need to tell you something," I said. He was ready to listen."Depending on how this goes, I may go off the deep end. If I do, just let me dive. I'll dive down deep but then I'll resurface shortly to get a breath and be fine after that. But I need that time off the deep end. If I spend too much time down there, I'll need you to pull me up however you can... I give you permission to shake me or slap my face (like in the movies), whatever it takes..."

The visit to the surgeon went as well as a visit to the surgeon goes to discuss treatment options you'd rather not have to decide upon regarding a cancer you'd rather not have, if it were up to you. As we sat there I had all my questions written out (thank you, Val Piazza, for prepping me on what to ask!). The doctor said that clearly I was "integrated" and

18

was of sound mind, not overly emotional, and able to hear what he was saying. He validated Pete's presence, as it often takes more than one set of ears to take away the full message a doctor is sending in this type of situation. So Pete and I left there with this information: The tumor is an invasive ductal carcinoma, grade 2, triple-negative. Options from a surgical standpoint would be lumpectomy with referral for chemotherapy and radiation, or, mastectomy with referral for chemotherapy.

For those unfamiliar with breast cancer, as I was for the most part, I'll explain from my limited knowledge. The tumor is first identified as ductal or lobular. Simply put, "ductal" is a cancer that starts in the milk ducts and "lobular" is a cancer that starts in the milk-producing glands (lobules).

Secondly, the tumor is graded 1, 2, or 3. A tissue sample graded a "1" means that the sample still looks mostly normal, and a grade of "3" means the sample looks mostly abnormal.

Finally, they test the sample for "receptors." A tumor is typically receptive (it grows in response) to the hormones estrogen and progesterone or a protein called human epidural growth factor receptor (Her2/ neu). A very small percentage of breast cancers prove to be a triple negative where the tumor is not found to be receptive to any of the above. A majority of breast cancers are estrogen and progesterone positive; a small percentage is Her2 positive; and an even smaller percentage is found to be triple negative. While Her2 positive tends to be a more aggressive type of cancer, treatment is more easily targeted, leading to better outcomes than in a triple negative tumor.I didn't take a dive that day. We both left the office feeling "okay" and truly just thankful for some answers and clarification as to what exactly we were dealing with. I didn't bother to look over the copy of the report the doctor had given at my request that night.

The next day, however, I poured over it and compared it with my mother's report from a year earlier (different doctor, different type of report). It was then that I noticed that my report said something different from what the doctor had told us in his office. I was confused (again) and texted a picture of the report to Val (thanks again, Val!) for confirmation that I was not reading it wrong. She confirmed that indeed I was not reading it wrong. I determined that first thing Monday morning I would be calling the surgeon's office for further clarification.

But I didn't have to wait that long. He called me on Saturday morning to explain he had been looking over my report and found his error. He wanted to be certain to correct this information with me. He also wondered if the second opinion I had scheduled at the University of Chicago at the end of the month could possibly be moved up at all. I assured him I would look into it. I had the final word as to the tumor's receptor: Her2 positive.

That was the doctor's final word on the subject, but ultimately, I know *Who* has the final word in every aspect of my life, and my trust remains in Him. Acts 17:28 says, "In Him we live and move and have our being."

With a couple of days behind me, time to think and

—

20

rethink, to actually take in and allow myself to feel and connect to all of the information given to me in the past week...today was my day to take the dive. I didn't go off the deep end to leave my family and faith behind. I just needed some time in my bed, under the covers to let it out. The nervousness, the sadness, the questions...they were all there, down deep. Pete sat beside me, ready with a hug, a nudge, a well-played sarcastic comment, and just his presence, silent support.

I swam around down there a little bit but it didn't take me long to resurface and breathe deeply again, because even down deep, God's presence and promises were there. "And He said to me, 'My grace is sufficient for you, for my power is made perfect in weakness.' Therefore I will boast all the more gladly about my weaknesses, so that Christ's power may rest on me... For when I am weak, then am I strong.'" 2 Corinthians 12:9-10.

2/17/15
Choose Peace

I started writing about choosing peace last June and decided to pick it up and finish it today. I was feeling overwhelmed then, and while I have the opportunity to feel overwhelmed today, I reflect on the lessons I've learned and choose a different response. I've formatted all older entries from here on in bold for distinction.

Written August 2014:

After my mom was diagnosed with cancer and she and my father calmly chose to manage the disease with diet, exercise, and a natural healing protocol, I was at a loss. Any part of my experience with cancer has been to as quickly as possible get to an oncologist, get the chemotherapy ball rolling, and schedule any surgeries that may be necessary while you're at it. My parents did not take such action and I was dumbfounded. It felt like I was going to have to learn to really let go and begin the process of saying goodbye.

Since that time I have seen my mother's determination and discipline to follow a strict diet and live a consistently active life. We have seen reports of cancer counts diminishing (to almost 0 at last count!) and have viewed scan results to show the mass drastically decreased. It has been a journey of not only wellness, but of faith.

When you or someone you love is dealt a life-changing blow, it can wreak havoc with your emotions. Your world is in upheaval and you question everything... But this time was different. My parents responded with such serenity and clarity and calm that I found the storm of my emotions diminishing to match. I realized that in some respects I was even working myself up because I thought, "My mother has cancer, why aren't I more upset all the time?!" But as I made my way through the difficult first months after her diagnosis, I came to a stark realization: *Just because there is drama in my life does not mean I need to respond dramatically.*

Drumming up emotion because it seemed like the appropriate response to a situation didn't make sense. If the waters of my emotions were tranquil and calm, why was I trying to stir them up? So I chose and do choose peace, as my parents have.

Now it is I who face an unwelcome diagnosis. I am choosing peace on a daily, sometimes hourly, basis following the path of serenity my parents have laid before me. My journey down this path may be different from what it has been for them, but I am weighing my options for medical care, treatment, etc., and remain calm while I consider all information. I am using natural means of addressing the cancer immediately while waiting to meet with specialists/surgeons at University of Chicago next week and the naturopath at the Osher Center for Integrative Medicine at Northwestern tomorrow. No matter what I learn at these appointments, I have determined not to make a decision based on fear. As my mother has instructed me from the very start of this process, "You need to go where the peace is."

"May the God of hope fill you with all joy and peace as you trust in Him, so that you may overflow with hope by the power of the Holy Spirit." Romans 15:13.

2/25/15
Hearing Voices

A friend posted the following Scripture on Facebook earlier this week (thanks, Ami) and I've been holding on to it for the past few days: "Whether you turn to the right or to the left you will hear a voice behind you saying, 'This is the way, walk in it.'" Isaiah 30:21

In this time of information gathering and just listening, I've been waiting to hear that Voice. There have been a lot of voices lately, but I'm seeking the peace to move forward, as my mom so wisely encouraged me to do. My husband is faithfully and patiently accompanying me to any and every person I can think of to ask or seek advice from since being diagnosed with invasive ductal carcinoma (breast cancer) earlier this month. This last week has truly been a roller coaster as I've visited a naturopath, a surgeon, a naprapath, and have shot off a number of emails to other people I wanted to hear from in regards to their treatment and experience. I've been devastated after sitting in offices where

health care professionals discuss their treatment plans that
include chemotherapy, radiation, and mastectomy. I've been
hopeful while sitting with natural medicine practitioners who
have seen the healing power of foods, supplements, exercise,
and a positive attitude. (These are all things that I am
currently utilizing.)

If I am honest it scares me to think about having chemo
and introducing more toxins into my body. It seems so
counterintuitive to subject myself to that. I've had
chemotherapy before and know it is a treatment that is very
difficult on the body. On the flip side, the thought of not
going through chemotherapy scares me. It is standard
medical treatment and in some respects, I think people would
consider me crazy for not following medical advice. So:
chemo, scary; no chemo, scary.

Then there's the topic of surgery. I've had so many
surgeries in my lifetime. The idea of another surgery is
unwelcome, to say the least. In the course of the many
discussions I've had and things I've read, the surgery aspect
of the proposed medical treatment is a preventative measure
in hopes of reducing the risk for recurrence. From anything
I've read or from what I understand, cancer can't simply be
"cut out" anyway.

So there you have it. I'm wrestling with all of the voices
that continue to speak their truth to me. The medical doctors
are speaking from what they understand, and the natural care
professionals are speaking from what they understand.
Everyone I've encountered seems well intentioned and

concerned.

"Whether you turn to the right or to the left, you will hear a Voice behind you saying, 'this is the way, walk in it.'" I'm waiting to hear *that* Voice.

3/2/15
I Am Doing Something

I had a difficult appointment at the University of Chicago on February 24, 2015. I left there feeling devastated. It wasn't the experience I had hoped to have, and I felt discouraged, as though I may never find the right health care team for me.

I've been in what I have termed the "information gathering stage" and the "team building stage" for a little bit now. It has been an important process but has begun to weigh on me. A couple days ago, I was so wound up and bound up in all the information and frustration that I couldn't see straight. Then, a friend suggested I talk to one of her friends (thank you, Kate!) and it was a Godsend. This new friend and I had a long conversation late into the night (thank you, Jori!) and she shared with me her journey navigating the rocky waters of breast cancer diagnosis, treatment, surgery, and the whole nine yards. The similarities between the two of us made the conversation that much more encouraging and informative. I felt so light and even joyous by the end of the conversation. I had a sense of direction! Even Pete commented on how good

I sounded when I was able to share with him the conversation and my thoughts as a result.

At this time, I have an appointment scheduled at The Block Center for Integrative Cancer Treatment on March 11, and I have a couple other professional individuals I would like to confer with, and then I'll make a final decision regarding a treatment team/ plan. I believe I already have this in my mind, but need to have these other conversations for confirmation. As I wait for these final conversations, I think about the steps I have already taken since the possibility of cancer came into being.

My mom arrived at my house on the day that I received "the call" and immediately began to lead me along to make caring for myself a priority right now. This is something I've struggled with in the past and know now more than ever, this needs to change. So while it may seem as though I'm taking a long time to "do something" to deal with this diagnosis, I want you to know I *am* doing something.

My focus has been on changing my environment. This involves a number of things. First, I'm changing the environment within my body from a toxic to a balanced one through the use of supplements and a strong nutritional plan. Dr. Terry Wahls has an excellent Ted Talk called "Minding Your Mitochondria" from which I've taken a lot of my ideas for green smoothie ingredients. I've cut out refined sugar and starches/ breads. My blood sugar is so well managed now. That is one of the fringe benefits.

The environment of the mind is constantly "under construction." We, all of us, are ever growing, learning, changing, and so that environment is an evolving one. The mind can, however, have consistent overtones of positivity or negativity, anger or peace, faith or doubt. I have been focusing on responding in a positive manner in all situations, managing my anger to remain calm/peaceful, and pressing in to my faith to manage the fear and doubt that would threaten to creep in at such a time as this. I'm learning to maintain a positive, healthy environment in my mind.

And finally, I'm making changes to my external environment. This effort has led me to two specific tasks: de-cluttering and organization. I've always been fairly organized but have been working on becoming more so, especially now that I am juggling doctors' appointments and very soon, treatment with two jobs and a family. Organizing my medical records/information has been a worthy project that not only serves to prepare me for upcoming appointments but also has de-cluttered my living space. In the arena of de-cluttering, I am learning to throw things away, recycle what I can, and to donate as much as possible. When there's less to fuss over in my immediate space, I am more likely to take a moment to relax.

That is the abbreviated version of what I am doing. I am preparing myself mentally, physically, emotionally, and spiritually for the long haul in this cancer treatment process. I intend to be a more peaceful, healthier, and happier individual—period.

—

30

3/5/15
Tsunami

One important warning sign of a tsunami is the vacuum effect. When the trough, or the low point of the wave, is reaching shore, it sucks coastal water seaward, exposing the sea floor. Within about five minutes or so after this recession, the wave's crest and its enormous volume of water crashes onto the shore. Tsunamis typically come in a series of waves, not just one big sweeping wave.

This week has been my emotional tsunami. The past month, I have "sucked it up" and seen the water line recede, exposing some of the sea floor. Well, this week the waves have come crashing down.

I came home from work sick on Tuesday. Frustrating. I need all vacation time saved up for when treatments begin. As of today, I'm still not feeling well and can't do much around here. I don't like this. However, being weakened physically I believe allowed the wave of emotions to break so that I would/could actually get in touch with all that the past month has meant.

I sobbed in grief over the loss of health once again, the inability to care for my family the way I'd like to, the thought of not being here with my family at all. I've been through the "cancer diagnosis" grief process before but this is a different experience. At age seventeen, when I was diagnosed with bone cancer, I grieved the loss of independence, health, and being able to remain an active part of my social community at school. Now I have a husband and little people in my life to think about, and that adds a whole new dimension to this process. Not only that, but the type of cancer I've been diagnosed with this time requires a different type of coping. Aside from emotional coping, bone cancer called for quite a bit of physical coping. Surgeries, physical therapy, weeks on crutches, and pain were all the work of bone cancer. Breast cancer is a different thing altogether. It impacts the very aspect of your image and identity as a female human being. I'm sure there will be more I have to say about that as time goes by.

I've been reading some of the things I wrote when going through bone cancer treatment, trying to draw strength and encouragement from my seventeen-year-old self. The following was written just a couple weeks after my eighteenth birthday, also a couple weeks after my limb salvage surgery to remove the tumor from my femur. I didn't know then that it would one day serve to encourage me at the point of another cancer diagnosis.

Written November 25, 1991

A whole month has gone by and all I have to say is, "I missed it!" That could be considered a blessing to me since I don't have anything *fun* to occupy my time. Nothing aside from fighting for my life and sanity, which at times seem so far out of my reach I wonder if I can call them my own!

To some my situation could seem sad: a nice, young girl having to suffer with such a disease as cancer, weeks on end away from home and stuck in a hospital. As for me, I consider it a blessing...and sad too. It is sad for *anyone* to have to suffer in such a way. Yet, as we are weak, our God is strong and will so strengthen us. God reveals Himself in His precious time. When the hours on a clock mean nothing, and a millennium is the twinkling of an eye. He may come slowly. He may come now. The fact remains, whether a year or a day —He will answer your call.

I sent these thoughts to my friend Steve to try and comfort him in a hard time. I wrote it; now I have to believe it. I do believe it in my heart, but to live that truth..."

And so, here I am, in the midst of this emotional tsunami, trying to live that truth. I will continue to share it for encouragement and comfort. I'm not the only one in this world who is going through something. We all have "something." So even as we hold on to our Rock in the midst of the waves, let's believe together that God will reveal Himself and will answer our call.

3/8/15
Learning to Regard My Body as More Than a Vehicle

I tell Pete quite often that he is a hard worker, and he is. I want him to know, through my words, that I recognize this and appreciate this about him. He is a very driven and focused individual and the proof of his efforts are in his work. It's something I not only appreciate but also really admire about him.

I've been sick for over four days. Until yesterday, Saturday night, I hadn't moved much from my bed since Tuesday morning. Once I was able to move again, I really moved. After wiping off the dining room table and sweeping the kitchen floor, I thought to myself, "You're a hard worker." I do believe this is the first time in perhaps *forever* that I've allowed myself that compliment.

While I accepted this compliment at the moment my inner self spoke it, I have been reflecting on it since. It has caused me to realize—or perhaps I knew it already but am now ready to fully admit—I am not good at caring for myself. I am indeed a hard worker, but what I'm now fully aware of is that I don't know when to shut it off. I may have admitted the lack of self-care before; however, I am now prepared to take steps toward change.

I love the memes on Facebook that say things like "Men, if you want to know how women think, imagine 1,254 browser pages open all at once ALL THE TIME." I also like the "I'm Going to Bed" list for men and women. "Men: go to bed. Women: wipe down the kitchen, tuck the kids in again, feed the dog, check the thermostat, check the door locks, throw in a load of laundry, clean the bathroom sink, clean the nightstand, go to bed." After reading some of these things, I confess: that is me. And, it is supremely difficult for me to "shut off."

It's easy to be critical of the workaholic who is away from home more often than not. What about the workaholic who's home but constantly doing something? This I would justify by saying, "It needs to get done." Or, "I want to do it so Pete doesn't have to after a long day at work." Or, on my weaker days, "If I don't do it, who will?"

It just so happens, a seed of self-care was planted as I sat in session with one of my clients several weeks ago. I was leading him in a relaxation exercise and closed with a meditation. He deals with chronic pain, so I wanted to share a positive thought on the body.

From Julia Cameron's book *Blessings*, I read the following:

"My body is more than just a vehicle that carries me through life. My body is a storehouse for my memories, a sensitive radar kit, which warns me of danger, a wise teacher who signals me how best to care for my spirit. When I take seriously the guidance it offers, I make decisions, which honor me in a holistic way."

Practicing self-care is something my husband and my mother, especially, try to stress with me. My friend Cindy also gives me kind lectures on the importance of this practice. I was listening but not hearing what they were saying. After receiving the news I did last month, another cancer diagnosis, and being sick for what seems like the fifth time since winter began, I realized it was (finally) time to listen, to take it seriously. The quote above returned to my mind. At the end of one short day of being able to keep food in me after days without, I was running my body like a machine, a vehicle, and I was not being kind. In my mind, I was full speed ahead, getting it done. As I considered this later, I reminded myself that there would *always* be something that needs to get done. It's in those "full throttle" moments that I must recognize it's more important to sit down with my sons and read a book instead of straightening the bookshelf.

Over the past few months, I have been making efforts to delegate more of the housework: practicing what I preach to my clients when we talk about family plans that include children's chores. Our boys, while young, are very helpful and very eager to be given tasks when there is work to be done. I know it's important to involve them now so that we will continue to work together as a family over the years. This is an act of teaching, togetherness, and caring for myself.

My body is more than a vehicle: it's a storehouse of memories, a library of wisdom, a partner through the most rewarding and tragic events of our time.

The meditation goes on to say: "I bless my body for its patient endurance, its mercurial intuition, and its persistence in speaking to me even when I slough aside the guidance it bears. My body is the most loyal of friends. I bless my body for its loyal companionship and commit to regarding it with tender care."

I do so commit. I talk to my clients about being kind through the way they talk to themselves. But, I think a very important piece is also the way we treat our physical self. While it's been easy for me to coach others in that direction of self-care, it hasn't been something I've practiced on a consistent basis. I bless my body for its patience and do commit to regarding it with tender care.

3/11/15
Treatment Plans
and the Importance of Today

There are days in my life that I would be happy to repeat. My wedding day, for one! It was like living the excitement of a thousand childhood Christmas Eves! Spending our first night together as husband and wife. The day I found out I was pregnant with our first child. The day I found out I was pregnant with our second *and* third at once! And of course, the day I found out I was pregnant with our fourth and final child. Meeting said babes for the first time. Those were great days, stellar moments in my life.

Conversely, there are days I have lived through that I would never care to repeat and even some that I may want to forget. Those days are marked by traumatic circumstances or the consequences of poor decisions. In life, however, we don't get the option to repeat or to forget. But through it all, I've learned some things. I realized if I get stuck in the memories of days gone by, the ones I'd ask to repeat, I risk missing out on the beauty of today and the memories that are being made here and now.

In the same respect, when I'm in the midst of a day I'd like to forget and am wishing time away, there is that same risk of missing out on the secret beauty that lies within. Not only that, but I may fail to see the beauty that lies within or beyond my struggle or trial. I have seen it time and again in my life, seen good things come from difficult situations.

Isaiah 61:3 says we will be given "...a crown of beauty instead of ashes, the oil of joy instead of mourning, and a garment of praise instead of a spirit of despair."

I was talking with a patient during a visit the other day. She asked me after some conversation how long I've been cancer-free. I briefly explained that it has been almost twenty-three years, but that I was recently diagnosed with breast cancer. She couldn't believe it. I told her that I see it all as a learning experience, adding, "There must be something I missed the first time so I hope to learn that lesson this time around!" And while we laughed about it at the time, I realize there is much truth to that. While I never wanted to have to repeat those days of cancer, chemo, and illness, there was much beauty and many positive things that came from that time, rich life lessons learned.

Today was my "big day" at The Block Center in Skokie. This is an integrative cancer care center. I met with a dietician for meal/supplement planning; a social worker for stress management and support planning; a medical technician for strength testing and vitals; an oncologist to develop a treatment plan; and a phlebotomist who took much of my blood for testing. It was a very busy, very productive day and here is the treatment plan: next week will be the week of tests—a PET scan to see if the cancer has spread anywhere else in my body and a MUGA scan to test my heart function. I will be having a port placed on March 24, early in the morning. This is an outpatient surgery. The port is inserted under the skin and a tube is looped into an artery for distribution of chemotherapy. This is preferable to using veins for chemo delivery. After the port placement, I will be going to the Block Center for blood work to see if I am cleared for chemotherapy and will be meeting with Dr. Block. If all goes well, I will receive a high dose of Vitamin C in preparation for chemo and will start chemotherapy the very next day. The day after the chemo treatment, I will go back to The Block Center for a Neulasta (white blood cell booster) shot and another dose of Vitamin C. This will happen every three weeks for six cycles. While it sounds arduous, I was very happy with every person I met at The Center today and am happy to have them for my healthcare team.

The Center itself is fairly small, very clean, and inviting. They offer yoga classes, cooking classes, and massage therapy all while you are there for your treatments. The program and the Center itself is set up in such a way that I actually felt like I wanted to spend time there. If one must have chemotherapy, it seems a very positive thing to have a space to go to that is so welcoming. So, while these things encourage me, I am also nervous. I hope I'm up to the task. I have excellent friend/family support, a healthcare team I like, and have confidence in and believe in a God who not only heals but also redeems even the darkest of situations/times.

In his book *The Making of an Ordinary Saint*, Nathan Foster says, "Weakness creates space for God. The healthy don't need a doctor." And so in this trying time, I plan to see God in the space created by my weakness. I plan to receive joy to replace my mourning. I am determined to find the beauty in each day, living moment by moment so that I don't miss a thing. There is beauty within and beauty beyond these difficult times and I plan to experience it all.

3/20/15
Healing Comes

Results of my PET scan were favorable. There was no sign of cancer anywhere else in my body besides the tumors in my right breast and one lymph node. Everything reported were things we already knew about. That was, and is, so encouraging!

I know there were some friends and family praying that there would be no cancer evident at all; a complete healing. While I think that would have been excellent, I have come to learn through my years and experience with a previous cancer, diagnosis of diabetes, and whatever else I've had to deal with along the way that "healing" doesn't always meet our expectations.

I've had many years to contemplate my thoughts and beliefs on this subject. When I was seventeen years old and diagnosed with cancer for the first time, osteogenic sarcoma in the left femur, after getting through the utter shock of it, I did pray, believing God could heal me in a heartbeat. Weeks passed, months passed, and I still believed He could heal me, heal me by taking away the cancer altogether and keep me from having to complete my forty-nine rounds of chemotherapy treatment. I knew He could mend my leg so that I wouldn't have to have limb salvage surgery and live with chronic pain and titanium rods in my leg. He, the Creator of my leg, could easily have taken a breath and crafted a new bone for me. But that didn't happen. And I completed my forty-nine rounds of chemo, had the limb salvage surgery, and since then deal with pain when I overdo it, the weather is off, or just because. But healing did come. Not the wow-factor kind, or the science-can't-explain-it kind, but the slow-born healing of medicine, treatment, and time. I had lived twenty-two years and seven months free of cancer! I remain a survivor of bone cancer and will celebrate that twenty-third anniversary on June 2, 2015 (as well as my ninth wedding anniversary that same day!).

I do believe in a miracle-performing, ever- present, all-concerning and consuming God who knows me intimately and infinitely, who loves me more than I can fathom. I believe He wants good for me. His primary concern is that I would know Him and would respond to His love. Oftentimes we want, hope, or expect that God is concerned about our comfort and happiness. And while I know and do believe that He loves to give good gifts to His children, those gifts don't necessarily correlate with our ideas of comfort and happiness.

A. W. Tozer said, "When I understand that everything happening to me is to make me more Christ-like, it resolves a great deal of anxiety." And honestly, I'm beginning to feel that way too. The amount of peace and clarity that has come already in this cancer diagnosis/treatment process has been incredible. I'm not comfortable but I'm peaceful.

As I consider this topic of healing in other areas of my life, not just cancer, I immediately think of anxiety. Starting in 2005, I was plagued by crippling panic attacks. I was unable to drive three miles without having to pull over, practice my deep breathing, and try to talk myself "off the ledge," so to speak. I was having panic attacks daily at work and could not go to the grocery store by myself for fear of getting stuck there, unable to move. The panic attacks subsided a bit amidst the joy and excitement of meeting Pete, falling in love with him, and ultimately marrying him.

In the midst of all of that anxiety I met Pete, got engaged, and planned a wedding—all in nine months! Obviously, there was some amount of peace and clarity experienced in the midst of that storm. Shortly after we were married, however, the panic attacks picked back up in intensity. One day I found myself sitting on the floor in the middle of Target with a cart full of groceries and I was frantically trying to call anyone I could think of who could talk to me and help calm me down. When no one could be reached by phone, I used the cart to carry me out of the store, staring at the floor with every step, left the cart at the door, and made it to my car praying, "God help me, God help me," all the way. It was one of the worst moments of my life. If you've never experienced anxiety, or particularly, panic, it may be hard for you to understand what

I'm saying here. But, in those moments you literally think you are going to die, lose control, be lost in some way, have a heart attack, pass out, or any number of things you might imagine that would cause fear or terror.

I'm a Licensed Clinical Social Worker. I have a private practice where I teach people coping skills and ways to deal with their anxiety and panic. I knew what I was experiencing but couldn't see my way around it. I knew I needed medicinal intervention, and so for just over a year I went on anti-anxiety medication. I took my medication faithfully, practiced my relaxation techniques, worked on renewing my mind and recounting Scripture, cut down on the heavy metal music and caffeine intake, and became acutely aware of my triggers so I could fend off a panic attack before it started. I had to change jobs as I became aware that the position I was in (working as a therapist at a cancer support center) triggered my anxiety. That move was very hard for me, because the position I held there was my "dream job." After making the change, however, I noticed the panic decrease. This was a long process that is easy to sum up here but was not so easy to implement. It was a lot of hard work, but it paid off. It has now been years since I've had a panic attack and years since I've needed the aid of anti-anxiety medication. I am comfortable and confident in saying that I was healed from panic attacks.

After leaving the Cancer Support Center due to my anxiety/panic, I went to work for hospice. I know, it may sound strange that that should have been a positive switch for me, but it was. There was something about the certainty that I was there to help make a person's transition from this life to the next a little more comfortable and to support the family throughout the process as well that held a strange sort of stability for me. I didn't have to guess if someone was going to die; I knew eventually all my patients would, and I knew my role in the midst of it. I found peace in that.

One of the things that hospice workers speak about with families and patients is this idea of healing. Healing doesn't always meet our expectations. It is true that healing comes in many forms and at different times. In death, we find healing of a deeper and spiritual kind. We talk about this in our culture and may even be unaware that we are doing so. When someone dies, we say things like, "He's in a better place," or, "She's not suffering anymore." This speaks of the healing of the soul, no longer in turmoil, at peace. My hospice experience and these many conversations have helped to shape my thoughts and beliefs regarding healing, and I am thankful for it.

In February 2015, I wrote a blog post entitled "Choose Peace" where I recounted my emotional struggle with my mother's cancer diagnosis over a year ago. In that blog I stated, "Just because there is drama in my life doesn't mean I need to respond dramatically." When I consider that statement now, I shake my head and laugh a delighted laugh. For one historically prone to anxiety and panic, it is amazing to think that in the face of my mother's diagnosis, I came away with peace of a deeper kind than I'd ever known. If you read or reread the post, you'll see much of that was due to my mother's example.

I received such good news yesterday. No cancer anywhere else in my body except what we were already aware of. I'm so grateful. "No cancer anywhere" would have been amazing to hear too! I have a hope and a trust that my cancer healing will come, and in the meantime, I am being healed in other ways and in other areas of my life day by day.

3/24/15
Productive Partners: Faith and Doubt

Faith and doubt are not polar opposites. Faith and certainty may be more so. It wasn't certainty that propelled Peter out of the boat onto the stormy sea; it was faith in the Savior standing on the waves.Faith and doubt go hand in hand to motivate us to dig deeper, seek answers, take another step, go further, work harder, and to trust with reckless abandon.

I'm glad that I understand this about faith and doubt, because as I stand with my feet planted on the deck of the boat and the stormy sea rages about me, I am quite uncertain. With all the excitement last week of finalizing a treatment plan and preparing to get things started, this week has turned into anxious energy. My stomach is sending me a twisted message and I'm feeling seasick.

Deep breath in, exhale slowly. Yes, I've been practicing my deep breathing and my visualization, imagining chemotherapy as an army sent to war on my behalf to wipe out the enemy. I've been visualizing the healthy cells in my body being protected from the battle and growing in strength.

I've visualized the room where I'll receive my treatments and have seen God Himself there with open arms to hold me in these hours.

The sky is dark and the waves are high. My little boat is being rocked. But my heart and mind are calm. I wonder if this is what it was like for Peter as he stood on deck, his hair and face wet from the crashing waves, muscles tense from gripping the side of the ship, anxiety stirring in the pit of his stomach. But there, in the midst of the storm, on the darkest, angriest rolling wave a figure appears. I can imagine Peter wiping his eyes with his arm to try to see more clearly as he squints into the distance. Could it possibly be? How could it be? Is that Jesus on the waves? Dear God, that is Jesus on the waves.

"Jesus, if that's you, tell me to come to you," Peter shouts over the howling wind.

"Come," was the response.

One leg over the side of the boat and then another and Peter is walking. On. Water. He walked. The wind continued to whip around him, and the waves slapped against his body. He took his eyes off Jesus, "saw the wind," and was scared again. At that moment, he began to sink and cried out for help. He sank and Jesus pulled him up. But the point is he had faith to step out of the boat despite his doubt.

I'm seeing the angry storm right now, feeling the wind and being carried on those waves. I keep thinking about the last time I had chemotherapy and how utterly sick I was. There were very few medications that could keep me from being physically ill with each treatment. I don't want to go there again, and feel I cannot. But I will if I must. I will get up tomorrow and go into surgery. I will have chemotherapy on Wednesday. Regardless of how it makes me feel, I will dig deep and summon the fortitude to go back and do it again in three weeks. If I believe Jesus is on the waves with me, faith will propel me forward even in my doubt. Though my thoughts and feelings are conflicted, I will put faith and doubt to work for me, to motivate and move me. I will trust with reckless abandon despite the wind and the waves. I will keep my eyes fixed on Him.

3/26/15
Day One, Done!

7:00 a.m.: Rise and Shine! (Couldn't sleep more than three hours total last night due to gas pain, so I was already up when it was time to be up.)

8:30 a.m.: Up and Dressed, out the door. Enjoyed a hearty breakfast of eggs, turkey sausage, and whole grain toast. Pre-medicated with Decadron.

To The Block Center about nine-ish. Ten minutes on the treadmill for some detoxifying cardio! (At least ten minutes of cardio prior to a chemotherapy treatment reduces the toxicity of that treatment!)

Have my Scripture ready: "Let us approach God's throne of grace with confidence, so that we may receive mercy and find grace to help us in our time of need." Hebrews 4:16 (Thanks for that one, Amy!)

Have vital signs taken. Looking good! Have my mantra ready: "God in, cancer out!" (Thanks for that one, Jennifer!) Pre-medication (the "rescue drugs") started after 10:00 a.m.

Took pictures and sent photo updates, including silly pole dancing photo with IV pole. Drank water. Headed for the loo.

Prayed over chemo bag before the meds entered my body. Directed it to join my army already deployed to fight the cancer. Used visualization here for a targeted attack on the cancer.

Actual chemotherapy started after 11:00 a.m. Experienced a *slight* reaction to said chemo. More steroids given to keep airway open, and chemotherapy resumed successfully. This drug is given with cryotherapy (cold packs on hands and feet) to help prevent side effect of neuropathy.

Received Benadryl. Got sleepy. Drank water.Tried to stay awake during support group/ lunch and was successful even after a five-minute silent meditation!

Drank water. Took a trip to el baño.Wrote out two birthday cards and one encouragement card.

Played Scrabble® on iPhone with my fantastic hubby! Drank water. Updated my blog. Drank water.Tended to matters in the lavatory. More photo updates taken for family. (None from inside the bathroom!)

Played cards with my love. Nibbled on a snack. Drank water. Stomach started to hurt. Drank more water. Visited the water closet.

More updates to blog before returning to said water closet. Day of pre-medication, Taxotere, Herceptin, Perjeta, Carboplatin, steroids, etc. complete around 5:30 p.m. Left The Block Center feeling hungry and relieved. We prayed a prayer of gratitude for all of our friends, family, and

—

healthcare team who serve us, strengthen us, and are on this journey of healing along with us!

Enjoyed dinner with my love at the Original Pancake House. Ate slowly: one buckwheat pancake, half an egg, water.

Stomach still hurt but by bedtime, which was 7:30-ish. Pete rubbed my back for a while and it helped relieve stomach pain. Then rubbed my feet for relaxation. Such a wonderful caregiver, this man!

I was asleep before 9:30 p.m. but awakened before 12:30 a.m. by some girls yelling in the hallway. Took over an hour to get back to sleep, only to be awakened by them again around 3:30 a.m. and here I am, shopping online for scarves for cancer patients and typing away at 5:30 a.m., unable to get back to sleep. I'm feeling pretty good. No stomach pain — I praise God for this relief! The soreness in my chest from the port placement is going away. I look forward to actually showering this afternoon and that may help me feel even better!

As far as side effects go, I'm feeling very weak. I can tell my taste is changing already, as the rice cake with peanut butter I started eating at 12:30 a.m. tasted different when I finished it at 4:30 a.m. I have a slight pinkish tint to my face and neck. I'm wondering if that's just coincidental or perhaps is some kind of rash. I remember getting this when I took Adriamycin many years ago. My skin is not irritated; it is simply pink.

I'm also noticing a strange sensation in my fingers and

toes. I know neuropathy can be a side effect of Taxotere. From what I understand, this side effect *can be* long-term, but isn't always so, and The Block Center provides cryotherapy with the Taxotere, as I noted before, in hopes of preventing this side effect or reducing its overall effect. I, however, have decided I don't want neuropathy at all! So, I pass on that. And otherwise, I am doing just dandy!

In a few hours, we shall be heading back to The Block Center where I will receive IV Vitamin C for an immune system boost and my Neulasta shot to give my white blood cell count a boost as well. Then home!

Day One, done!

Written for me during my chemotherapy treatments by my friend, the late Lana Millbocker on 3/26/92.

Sarah

I would climb the highest mountain
Or swim the seven seas,
Just to show you how much
Your friendship means to me.
I would dig to the center of the earth
Or touch this very sky,
And if you told me to find a way
Through the heavens, I would fly.
For if you were the day and I the night
Close to you, I'd find a way to be near
I'd stop the earth from turning
And make all darkness disappear.
To lose you is my biggest fear
For people like you are few.
You have a heart so full of love
And a soul so strong and true.

3/26/15
Like A Tree

As I was sitting in the waiting room on Tuesday morning, March 24, contemplating the port placement procedure I was about to undergo, an overwhelming sense of grief began to overtake me. The realization of what this surgery means, what was about to begin for me, a trajectory set to a pace that I could not slow down...it was time to go and I wasn't ready.

"I feel like I'm saying goodbye to my body as I've known it," I told Pete, "just when I was starting to feel stronger and more at peace with the next phase of my body's life, beginning to truly appreciate the marks from childbirth and happy to move past those years to the next."

We chose to sit in silence, Pete with a quiet but steady hand on my knee. A metaphor I could visualize came to my mind. "*My body is like a tree marked by the events of time,*" I thought and wrote it down before they came to take me into the operating room.

As I reflected upon this thought the next day with Pete sitting next to me at The Block Center in a treatment pod named after a tree, and the chemotherapy drugs beginning their work inside me, I shared my thoughts with him about the changes and especially the marks that my body will bear in the coming months. I reiterated that I thought my body was like a tree marked by the events of time. When I said it, he knew instinctively that I was referring to the storms, fires, marks from car accidents, chopping, loss of limbs that leave stumps on the side of a tree, marks of a lifetime.

Without hesitation, he added, "Still standing. Providing comfort, shade, and beauty to the world, soaking up the light of the sun."

I sat silent at his words, tears filling my eyes. One can't really improve on that statement. What a generous and wise thing for a husband to say to a wife who is concerned about what chemicals, time, treatment, and surgeries will do to her body; how encouraging, loving, and reassuring.

Pete has said, in regard to the inevitable physical changes, "But I get you." Nothing else makes a difference in how he feels—no marks or weaknesses or changes. He gets to be with me and that's the most important thing. Period.

Considering my body as a tree, with all its dents, marks, glory, and splendor, reminded me of Jeremiah 17:7-8, used at the spiritual retreat Pete and I had just attended.

"But blessed is the one who trusts in the Lord, whose confidence is in Him. They will be like a tree planted by the water that sends out its roots by the stream. It does not fear when heat comes; its leaves are always green. It has no worries in a year of drought and never fails to produce fruit."

Looking at this Scripture once again in the light of the conversations with my husband and the thoughts of the previous days, I was once again encouraged. Even in the heat, fire, drought, those events of time, a tree planted deep has no fear, no worries, and will continue to bear fruit. So I also realized that even in the midst of my time of trouble, when I'm at my weakest, I remain one who is firmly planted in Faith, Hope, and Trust in the Lord, one who continues to live a fruitful life, and *that* is beautiful.

(He doesn't like selfies but he likes me so, here's a selfie.)
I'm so thankful for this man.

3/30/15
Pain and the Power of the Spoken Word

In my "I Am Doing Something" post last month, I talked about my efforts to change my environment to make my body inhospitable to cancer but also to clear my mind of negativity and fear. I've taken the latter a step further. I realize it's one thing to target my thoughts and yet another to tame the tongue, to become aware of and purposeful with my words.

Since starting chemotherapy last week and having lived the last few days in a painful fog from which I'm just now starting to emerge, this is proving to be more of a challenge for me. I want so badly to add an "I hate cancer" hash tag here or a "chemo sucks" there. I've refrained because here is what I believe: I believe our words have life-giving power. They have the power to bless or the power to curse. As Proverbs 18:21 says, "The tongue has the power of life and death…"

As I've worked on this in the last few weeks, I am in disbelief at some of the things I mutter under my breath. The words I say are reactionary words or statements, but I utter them nonetheless. Upon further reflection, I'm glad they are words or phrases that go mostly unheard by others, but I realize that if I speak them into being, whether they are heard directly or not, they still hold the same power. (Even if I'm the only one who hears...)

I would not want someone speaking words of negativity, pain, unrest, or worry over me as I am in the healing process, so why oh why would I speak those words over myself in a time of suffering? It is in the midst of that suffering and pain where I am in need of the most life-giving, positive, peaceful, encouraging language. In seeking this language to soothe and to heal, I am not diminishing my emotions or my suffering. I can freely admit that my head, face, mouth, and esophagus have been plagued with sores these last days and that I have been beyond exhausted to the point of being unable to maintain consciousness for a full three hours straight. It is not negativity that speaks when I recount that I have had stomach cramps and have had to fight for the energy to even talk to my kids, let alone play with them. And now, I am thankful to say that I am coming out of that cloud. I have more energy and have been able to stay awake all day today. I'm able to stand for several minutes at a time and have been able to eat a full meal.

In those difficult moments of the last few days, I told my husband that I felt defective and apologized for being unable to do much of anything. I learned that I am able to remain authentic and real about my situation while maintaining life-giving language because even in those dark moments, life-giving words came to my heart and mind. Pete would read to me from *Prayers from the Heart* by Richard J. Foster, to provide more words of encouragement, hope, and peace when I had no words.

One of the prayers he read is a very simple one from Lady Julian of Norwich. She shared that God, in His tender love, comforts all those trapped in pain and sin by speaking these words to them: "But all shall be well, and all shall be well, and all manner of things shall be well."

All shall be well. I want to absorb these words, to feel them at the core of my soul. All shall be well. And because I want to integrate these words into my being, I choose to use the language of life and blessing, of hope and truth. And I pray with King David of old, "May the words of my mouth and meditations of my heart be pleasing in your sight, Lord, my Rock and my Redeemer..." Psalm 19:14.

3/31/15
Growing Gracefully and
Knowledge of the Mutated Gene

I've wanted to write a book for many years now. The idea may have been conceived in English class at Cheboygan Area High School where Mrs. Pletcher indulged my love of writing and my belief that I had a way with words. It was one of my favorite times in a school day, going into her classroom to read the quote on the board, which was put there for us to respond to in our journals. If only I could find those journals from high school and take a look back at what sixteen- and seventeen-year-old Sarah had to say about some things. At that age, time seemed to move so slowly, and my thoughts and writings, anything I created, seemed to me to be larger than life. It was right about then, at what I perceived to be the peak of my confidence and creativity, that I was dealt a devastating blow. Cancer. I was diagnosed with osteogenic sarcoma, bone cancer, in the left femur and served one year of intensive chemotherapy at the University of Michigan's

Mott Children's Hospital in Ann Arbor, Michigan. My heart is in my throat as I recall sitting with my parents in a sterile office, leg in a cast from toes to hip one short day after a biopsy surgery, being educated on all of the chemo drugs I would be given and all of the horrendous side effects that have ever been reported through the life and use of each. I wanted to transfer myself to the other side of the window I was seated beside and to perch there on the ledge, sitting in the sunshine like one of those birds. Then, if I could fly away like them too... Instead, I sat there and cried. This was July 1991, a month before the start of my senior year of high school, a year that would largely be spent in the hospital. In that moment, I could not imagine how I would survive.

But I did survive. I not only survived, I also thrived. My initial instinct had been to recoil, to turn inward, circle the wagons and hunker down until the danger passed. Instead, I made friends. I reached out, nominated my mother and myself as the welcome committee orienting new patients to the oncology unit. I used humor and laughter, got to know the nurses, made light of the admission paperwork, was real with my doctor, learned to do "the bridge" while shuffling cards. I lived in community. Thank you, Channon Boullion and Tami Lickert Harrison, for being my dear friends and family, in sickness and in health, for being active parts of that community. What if I had recoiled? What if I had allowed cancer to shut me down? I would have missed the beauty that lies beyond cancer, beyond 1991, beyond the age of seventeen. At that time, it was like groping desperately, trying to grab something just out of reach as I tried to hold onto my senior year or the ages of seventeen and eighteen, then to grieve their loss from a hospital room. But there was beauty beyond the safety and comfort of my home in Northern Michigan that year, found in the friends and community in Ann Arbor hospitals.

It was an amazing, painstaking journey and a life-changing one. While creativity and writing had taken a bit of a back seat to dealing with side effects of treatment, trying to maintain schoolwork while in the hospital, and squeezing in as much of a social life as a compromised immune system would allow, my heart and soul turned to music for an outlet. One of my favorite bands in the 80s was a Christian rock band named White Heart. Their song "Desert Rose" became my theme song. I had a CD player in my room at all times. This was before the age of iPods and MP3 players. I also received cards and letters through the United States postal service, the hard copies that get delivered by a mailman requiring paper, envelopes, and stamps. This was before the day of email, or at least for me. I didn't have email until I went away to college.

Those days of life, bald and hospitalized, sick and unsure, the era of handwritten notes and face-to- face encounters, seem a lifetime ago. As I recall it now, it seems like a different world altogether.

Many years later—and with a lot of amazing and interesting things to happen in the meantime—I turned forty. I remember when my mom was forty. Actually, I can remember when my mom wasn't yet thirty! And there I was, turning forty, holding a three- month-old child in my arms. This babe, nothing short of a miracle, was not supposed to be. One of the side effects of each and every chemo drug I had taken (and had received a lifetime dose of within that year) reported the side effect of infertility. My son whom I held, my four sons surrounding me now, are each a God-given gift. It amazed me and completely baffled me. Where had time gone? How could I be so blessed?

And then I turned forty-one. I turned forty-one and I had not yet gotten over the fact that I had turned forty. It was a difficult transition for me, for some reason. We all see ourselves through misty, foggy, or distorted lenses. We judge ourselves based on criteria and expectations spoken over us when we are young or ideals we ourselves determined somewhere along the way. We take joking words or mindless spoken observations and make them important facts about us that must be reckoned with. For me, that was what it meant to turn forty-one. All of the "over the hill" jokes and "growing old gracefully" commercials were facts I was facing and I didn't feel gracious about it at all. In fact, I struggled.

Marriage and children had continued teaching the lessons of grace and love that I had known about through my parents' example and in theory during my earlier years. I tried to be a good student of life. I began to write again in order to gain perspective on my changing life and to share any insights or lessons learned with friends and family.

Soon, events would come about that would continue to

—

shape the way I felt about and experienced growth and change. It was January 2014 and my mom—Mimi to my children—was diagnosed with breast cancer. It was a shock and something that took me a long time to get a handle on. (Not to say I "handle it" at all times, but I have learned to be calm in the midst of the storm.) My parents displayed such a deep sense of peace and rest in the midst of this news. They prayed and waited and weighed all options before deciding on an all-natural approach to treating her cancer. This was not easy for me to accept. After all, when I was diagnosed with cancer, it was a matter of only two days before a port had been placed and chemo had started. I wondered where, then, was their sense of urgency. There is much more to the process and I've chronicled many of my thoughts and feelings in previous posts. But the long and short of it is, I watched as my mother very consistently and determinedly managed her diet, exercise, supplement regimen, and other forms of natural health care. I learned from her discipline and care of herself. I watched my father support her and love her deeply through researching her diagnosis and treatment options, and by staying close to her side through it all. (As I yelled from the sidelines, "Start chemo! Get a mastectomy! What are you waiting for?" I've since apologized for my frantics.)

It was probably around Christmas, 2014 when I came into the grace of growing. I believe there is grace for us every step of the way in our lives. When I say, "I came into the grace of growing," it is because this was a significant moment of change in my journey when I accepted "grace" for myself, grace as Webster's defines it is: "ease and suppleness of movement or bearing". At that time, I looked at my four beautiful boys playing together in our cozy living room, those healthy, happy, energetic children who were given as gifts to my husband Pete and me. Any lost sleep, stretch marks, C-section pain, or scars paled in the light of such a sight. Peaceful perspective. I began to recount all of the blessings in my life: healthy and loving family, faithful friends, employment, Church community, and the list went on. This was not the first moment of profound gratitude in my life. I've experienced that time and again. However, this moment held a specific message for me regarding growing and aging. My book was not yet written. This beautiful story of love and grace, of peace in the midst of storms, of blessings and babies, had many chapters yet to fill and in that moment, I experienced clarity and contentment at the realization of my place in life and time.

And it was around Christmastime that I had pain in my right breast. I imagined I had caught an elbow from one of those beautiful boys I reveled over at a Christmas gathering. The pain went away the next day, but a persistent husband asked me to follow up with the OB/GYN. I had my first mammogram, breast ultrasound, meeting with a surgeon, biopsy, and resulting cancer diagnosis soon after that visit.

I was admittedly a little bitter. Hadn't I just turned a corner emotionally, even perhaps matured a little in this journey of life? How could another cancer diagnosis be possible? I felt I had paid my dues to cancer. I admit, it was a tough pill to swallow, that diagnosis and subsequent weeks of doctors' appointments and treatment planning. There were moments I could not believe I was sitting in *that* office again having *this* conversation.

Last week I received my first chemo treatment at The Block Center in Skokie, IL. Following the example of my parents, Pete and I took time to gather information regarding my diagnosis and treatment options. It was an important process as we sought peace in the midst of decision-making and in the selection of our health care providers/treatment team. We found that peace at The Block Center where they take an integrative approach to cancer care. My nutrition, physical activity, and emotional state of mind were all considered, as well as the cancer diagnosis and conventional chemotherapy treatment. It was during this first treatment for my second primary cancer diagnosis that I learned that I have a mutated cancer-suppressor gene, a condition called Li-Fraumeni syndrome. I am just beginning to learn about this syndrome and what it means for my family and me. At this time, I understand that my risk for breast cancer with this genetic factor was 3 times the average risk. It puts a lot in perspective regarding the sarcoma I had in my teens and now the diagnosis of breast cancer at age forty-one.

Throughout this new stretch of road, yet another learning process, I will share my thoughts and experiences. My book is not yet finished. There are many more pages to fill. For now, I am present in this moment and have come to realize I am unable to handle anything more than that. I have found even praying for my "daily bread" to be a little overwhelming these days. My prayers have been moment by moment.

But I know there is beauty in each moment, each day. I know there is beauty beyond, around, and within a cancer diagnosis and a mutated gene. It is for me to see that beauty, to know it, experience it, and write about it. I haven't lost sight of the lessons I've learned and know that all the chapters I've lived to this day have served to inform and equip me. I will continue to grow gracefully and to share the beauty of this life.

4/5/15
All Things New

"He who was seated on the throne said, 'I am making everything new!' Then He said, 'Write this down, for these words are trustworthy and true.' He said to me: 'It is finished! I am the Alpha and the Omega, the Beginning and the End. To the thirsty I will give water as a gift from the spring of the water of life. Those who overcome will inherit all these things, and I will be their God and they will be my children.'" Revelation 21:5-7

It's Easter Sunday. Resurrection Day. Not only that, but it's springtime in the Midwest and we are enjoying milder weather, more hours of sunshine in each day, and the excitement of buds on trees and in our flowerbeds. As for me, I've been enjoying being able to eat without adverse effects for the first time since my chemo treatment one week and five days ago.

As I've been reflecting on all that this season means, not only spring but also Easter, remembering the resurrection of Christ, the above Scripture has remained constant in my mind. I love the image of new birth or rebirth this time of year illustrates so beautifully: birds make nests and lay eggs, little green shoots emerge from an otherwise barren-looking ground, and the dark trees of winter begin to show colors at the tips of their branches once again. It's such a glorious time of the life cycle and a very poignant one for me this year.

Since receiving the results of my genetic testing showing that I am positive for Li-Fraumeni Syndrome, I have felt a dark, heavy cloud hanging over me. While I would share the information with family and friends saying, "It's just providing information, it's not a diagnosis," it felt just the opposite. I realized I was taking the news of this mutated tumor suppressor gene and shackling myself to cancer for the rest of my life. It was as if I couldn't see a future.So, today, in light of and remembrance of Christ's work on the cross for salvation, His suffering for healing, and finally His return from the grave for life everlasting, I decided to claim the victory for myself! As the Scripture from Revelation 21 says, "...those who overcome will inherit the water of life. He is making all things new!" This proclamation and promise seemed to be a ray of light for me in a very dark place. Christ's victory is all the more sweet for me in the valley of the shadow of death.

I prayerfully revisited the genetic testing information this afternoon and found it to be less intimidating than I had remembered, and I found myself encouraged. Even if none of the information had changed, whether on paper or in my mind, it wouldn't have mattered because He who is on the throne says, "Behold! I am making all things new!" That doesn't mean my genetics will change or that I won't have cancer tomorrow. But I have the assurance of being made new, being given a renewed hope, experiencing the rebirth of determination and perseverance.

Yesterday I would have asked, "How can I do this?" Today the answer is, "He who is on the throne is making all things new!" So, for today, I claim a victory. I accept Christ's work on the cross and the power of His resurrection as part of my inheritance. I will hold to it in dark places. And in times of desperation or despair, I will look to the light of a new day.

4/9/15
Suffering Well

I'm listening to *Soul Surfer* on audiobook right now. It's the story of Bethany Hamilton, a young surfer girl in Hawaii who survived a shark attack but lost her left arm as a result. She shares the trauma and trials of the attack and rehabilitation but also her determination to continue surfing and competing. In the very first chapter of her book, Bethany said something I found to be quite profound. Hearing it was very timely for me after a day of emotional and spiritual struggle:

"I don't pretend to have the answers to why bad things happen to good people. But I know that God knows all those answers and sometimes He lets you know in this life and sometimes He asks you to wait so you can have a face to face talk about it."

My heart was heavy Monday. There are so many people I love who are going through such difficult things right now: bearing up under the weight of depression, walking the weary road of caring for a sick child, learning to live solo when a spouse leaves, facing the facts of a medical diagnosis, the untimely death of a loved one, dealing with the confusion and burden of infertility, striving to cope with chronic pain, the sadness of unfulfilled dreams, and the list goes on. I was truly questioning why such hard times would come to such good people. I'm thankful for the conversation I had with my coworker, Carol, that day. She reminded me how limited our view is and how our confusion and frustration should lead us to rely on God more because He sees the big picture.

I realize how limited my understanding is and do know that I see but a tiny puzzle piece of the big picture of life, time, and space. I needed to be reminded of this and to return my focus to God where I can depend on Him for guidance, and sometimes, answers.

While waiting in line at the grocery store later that day, I picked up a devotional that was on clearance and randomly opened the book. "Patient Perspective" was the name of the reading. I thoughtlessly read the thing, then put it back on the shelf. Walking to my car and for hours afterward I could not get that one-minute-read from *Everyday Prayers and Praises* out of my head. It said, in part: "If you're impatient for a situation to change, pray for perspective, do what you can, and then trust God for resolution in His time and in His way." This struck me and stuck with me to the point that I had to go back later and buy the book. Even now, as I reread this portion, it resonates within my very soul. I am reminded: I am not in control. In fact, I suffer more when I struggle for control, when I manipulate the words of my prayer in hopes of eliciting a certain response, or try to walk/talk/be just right so that good will come about. As if it even works that way!

When I realize my tendency toward actions such as these, it confuses me. Those things sound like the acts of a superstitious mind and I don't identify with that. Why then do I do it? I believe it goes back to this struggle for control in the midst of suffering or distress. I may not feel the need to totally avoid the suffering but I do desire to resolve it, to "fix" it for those I love.

I began to focus on the idea of suffering in this life. Everyone suffers. Some people may seem to "get off easy" if we compare, but there really is no use in comparing. In this life, we are all given our own road, our own journey. Sometimes we forget to look at the scenery and become focused on the bumps before us. I wasn't even focusing on my own bumps. It was everyone else's bumps that were getting me down! I pray and I pray so hard for some things, again, manufacturing phrases or words I hope will be the winning combination to achieve the resolution/ healing/deliverance/results I so desire. But I am confident it does not work that way.

I've decided that if I must suffer (and we all do/will), I'd prefer not to be frantic about it; I'd like to learn to suffer well. I've been reading different articles and blogs in regard to suffering. I found a sweet little blog post that gives practical advice for dealing with suffering. I'm providing the link here: http://natepyle.com/practices-for-suffering-well. I love what the author says about honesty in the midst of suffering and how freeing and healing it can be to simply acknowledge that we are suffering.

This memory came to my mind as I was wrestling with thoughts on suffering and my determination to suffer well. It provides a fair illustration of how this can be accomplished: to lie back, not giving up on the situation, but with purpose and determination to be at peace in the midst of pain. It can make the suffering somehow smoother.

It was the only time in my life when I thought I was going to die, literally. I've lived through car accidents that were scary; have been diagnosed with cancer twice; undergone numerous surgeries; traveled to countries not necessarily "safe" for women, among other things that may have put my life at risk in some way. But the only time I ever thought, "I'm going to die here," was while swimming in Hawaii. I was new to the ocean and having an amazing time swimming out on the waves, which were huge that day. It was so much fun rising up with a wave, being able to see so far and then to be lowered down again. After some time, I became very tired. Swimming and fresh air are a beautiful pair to make one fatigued. As I started for the shore I was hit from behind, or above, by a crashing wave. I was right at the breaking point, the place where the wave, after raising up high, crashes down before rolling into shore. I've never experienced such power of nature before. It drove me into the ground with such force I could feel my skin grating against the sandy ocean floor. Before I could gather my strength to pull up out of the

Finding Myself...Facing Cancer

water, another wave came crashing down on me with similar effect. I became frantic, flailing my arms and legs, struggling to hold my breath so I didn't inhale anymore salt water. My lungs and eyes were burning from the stuff. "I can't get out! I'm going to die!" I thought. Another wave broke on top of me and I was scraping bottom again. I knew I had to compose myself. In the midst of the panic something within me identified the rhythm of the waves and knew when the next break would be coming. I relaxed myself and allowed the break to pummel me into the sand once again as I determined to follow the drive of the wave in attempt to be propelled closer to shore and out of the breaking point. Maybe it was my presence of mind, maybe it was my determination, maybe it was the end of that set of waves and didn't have anything to do with me at all, but I found myself out of the proverbial wave-blender, battered and gasping for air as I crawled onto the shore—alive!

When I quit fighting the waves and literally rolled with them, the pain of being driven into the ground wasn't lessened but it was a smooth transition out of the break and I was able to move up out of the situation.

These thoughts have stayed with me throughout this week. This idea, this theme is not one that I've resolved within myself. Learning to suffer well, like anything else, is a process. I'm sure I will continue to grow in it and be challenged by it with each new trial. I am determined to pray for proper and patient perspective in the midst of difficulty, to relax under the weight of the waves and roll with the turbulent tide, and to focus on the One who knows the answers to the tough questions.

Letter written April 11, 1992 during chemotherapy treatment for osteogenic sarcoma, 8 months completed:

To the Evangelical Covenant Church:

Dear Congregation,

I would like to express my gratitude to you on behalf of my family and myself. We thank you for the support through cards, letters, thoughts, and prayers. We especially appreciate the use of your Safari minivan during this year of chemotherapy.

I also want to publicly thank God for all of His blessings through the past year. I have had a rough year, physically, emotionally, and mentally. I have struggled with losses and rejoiced in victories. I am happy to say that I have only 4 more treatments left until I am finished!

I know you all have been faithful in keeping me lifted in prayer: that is far better than any medicine. Praise God!

Thank you again.
Love in Christ, Sarah Fenlon and Family

1992   2015

4/12/15
My Boys

Once the decision had been made to begin chemotherapy treatments, I knew something would need to be said to our kids. I had cut my hair very short before treatment started, thinking this would make it less traumatic for both my boys and me when the hair actually did fall out. Bobby, five years old and our eldest son, was the only one to even notice my haircut at the time. Teddy and Sam, both four, didn't seem to notice the change. Of course, William at eighteen months, while in tune with my every movement, didn't seem the least bit thrown off by the pixie hairdo.

I sat all of the boys down one day and told them that I would be taking medicine that would make my hair fall out one day. They asked the usual, "Why?"

"Because some medicine just makes your hair fall out," was my simple reply. Then I made it interesting by adding, "So when my hair starts to fall out would you guys like to use the clippers to shave my head?" Everyone cheered with support and excitement for such an idea.

And so, the day has arrived. My hair actually started falling out a couple of days ago, but it was getting really annoying as of today. For me, my head gets really itchy when the hair starts the leaving/dying process. It becomes easy to pull hair straight out. This evening, I gathered my guys together in the bathroom and showed them how easily hair could be pulled out of my head. I let each of them try it if they wanted to. They weren't as eager as I had anticipated. Sam, one of my four-year-olds, was the most interested in trying to pull my hair out. Bobby and Teddy were a little timid about it.

Next, I bent over a towel and combed out as much of my hair as I could. I reminisced about the evening in 1991 when I did the same thing in the bathroom of my home in Cheboygan, Michigan. My hair had been longer then, and it was much easier to get a grip on the hair to get it out. After that process I had ended up looking like a balding middle-aged man and got some laughs out of my siblings when I re-enacted Chris Farley's Middle-Aged Man character from *Saturday Night Live*. Then my dad had taken a Bic razor and shaving cream to my head to finish the job.

When it came time to use the clippers this evening, everyone volunteered to be first. Bobby was the first in line. I guided his little hand while he held the clippers and made the first sweep down the middle of my head. He wanted to try it for himself so I let him have a go. He did a pretty good job of getting a couple rows started. Sam went next. He was very serious as he held the clippers and went slowly about his work. Then there was Teddy. He was afraid he was going to hurt me, and after I assured him that he couldn't hurt me, he set about shaving away. He even laughed a little. My boys took a couple more turns and then it was Dad's turn. Pete came in and Bobby took my camera to catch a few shots of Dad finishing up Mom's haircut. I took the clippers to my own head in the end, just to get the finer or more blonde strands of hair that my guys may have missed. All in all, it really was a fun family experience and a true bonding time, in my estimation.

Afterward, Bobby laughed at me and said I looked funny without hair, but I know he'll get used to it. William, our toddler who was not present during the shaving (by design because that boy is into everything!), didn't bat an eye when I came into my room to give him a kiss once the deed was done. I had wondered if my extreme new look might weird him out, but no.

All in all, my fellas have been amazing throughout our cancer journey. We have not used the word "cancer" with them, mostly because that would be too difficult to explain. I haven't even said "I'm sick" or anything of the sort. I told them about the medicine I'm taking (chemo) and they knew after the first treatment that I wasn't feeling well. They were so sweet. For days after my treatment, they would pay special attention to me.

"Are you feeling better, mom?""Would soup and salad

make you feel better?" "Do you feel better now?" "What will make you feel better?" They would ask these questions almost daily. I would get extra hugs, kisses, and pats on the hand, head, or back from them. Boys are so sweet on their moms! I could sense their love and care for me and it just touched my heart.

The last five days have been good ones, where I am up and able to do all of my usual "duties." As a result, I haven't had the extra-special treatment. I'm positive these boys are very in tune with what is happening here and they have journeyed right along with us and have been such amazing supports to this mama.

Teddy and Sam have a banana every morning. They like the bananas with the stickers on them, which they call "sticker bananas." As you know, not every banana comes with a sticker on it so sometimes this can cause difficulty for us.

"Here, Mom," Sam would say, offering me the sticker from his banana, "Because I love you."

Heart melts here.

Both Teddy and Sam have been saving their stickers for me, making sure I know they're thinking of me and that I'm clear about how much they love me. I know, boys. I know.

I am so blessed by these four little men. Bobby encourages me with his extra hugs and availability to help. Teddy uplifts me with his sense of humor and extra squeezes.

Sam warms me with his many kisses and concern. William cheers me with his celebration every time I come home or enter the room. I have come to see more clearly than ever before that these four boys are love letters from God to me. Message received (and how!).

4/12/15
Becoming Through Suffering

At the beginning of March, Pete and I were finishing up a conference, which I refer to as our spiritual retreat. Presenting at this spiritual retreat were Richard and Nathan Foster, father and son teachers, authors and speakers. Richard Foster wrote a book in the 1970s called *The Celebration of Discipline*. Nathan took that book, in which Richard outlines twelve spiritual disciplines, and tried to purposefully/intentionally practice each one. This process took him four years, and he compiled his experiences into a book, *The Making of an Ordinary Saint*. These two works were the basis of this retreat.

I've shared this before, but the opening scripture was found in Jeremiah 17: 7-8, "But blessed is the one who trusts in the Lord, whose confidence is in Him. They will be like a tree planted by the water that sends out its roots by the stream. It does not fear when heat comes; its leaves are always green. It has no worries in a year of drought and never fails to produce fruit."

This idea of the heat and the time of drought was used to illustrate a time of suffering, doubt, or trial. Throughout the conference, the theme of suffering was reiterated.

A couple weeks ago, I had a wonderfully uplifting conversation with a friend of mine, Chaplain Carole. I was telling her about the spiritual retreat and trying to recount what I had learned. I told her about this theme of suffering. Not just suffering in and of itself, but suffering as formation or formation through suffering. God redeems what seems like lost time or pointless pain. Our suffering is not in vain. Through our pain and suffering, we are forced to press on and keep going. We can learn more about ourselves, faith, God, and others at our point of pain. Our character is shaped and developed in trials and by fire. I don't want my suffering to be meaningless. I want to "become" something through my suffering. Even in times of heat and drought, I want to have a fruitful life.

I had a MUGA scan the week before beginning chemotherapy. It is when radioactive tracers are mixed in with a sample of your blood, then injected into the arm. The blood sample with the tracer heads straight for the heart; the scan then captures pictures of the function of the heart. Well, in order to take the blood sample and to inject it requires a couple needle stings. The blood draw was a quick prick and for a moment I found myself wishing I didn't have to feel it. *Isn't there something they could give to numb a person's arm before doing that?* I thought.

As I lay on the table a bit later to have the blood and tracers injected back into my arm, another thought came to me. *It's just when we numb out and simply decline to embrace all that our journey has to hold that we become angry or bitter.*

So when I knew the next needle sting would be coming, I took a deep breath and tried to simply absorb the pain. In perspective, I can imagine it would be much harder to do this with a deeper, lengthier, and more intense pain than a needle stick. But the point is, numbing out doesn't work anyway; it goes against the grain of experience, the same way denial does. If I say, "It doesn't hurt," I'm lying to you but I'm also robbing myself of the fullness of that experience. Pain and suffering are part of the human story.

I wish I could say that the second needle sting that I tried to absorb and embrace didn't hurt as much as the first, but that would be inaccurate. It did hurt, but my attitude, intention, and overall emotional experience of that needle stick was different from the first. So I realize my intention and attitude play a large part in how I am able to bear pain.

I'm talking about physical pain here. But I've found the same principles to be true regarding emotional or spiritual pain and suffering. Not only that, but I know I do not enter the Valley of the Shadow of Death alone. No temptation, concern, pain, irritation, frustration, threat, illness, nothing, nothing, absolutely nothing can separate me from the love of God. I do not go alone. I do not suffer alone. And I know that, despite these trials, my soul will receive nourishment from a loving God, and because of it I will continue on and become more.

4/15/15
Don't Worry, (Make Yourself) Be Happy

Don't Worry...

Day 0What a beautiful morning! The sun was shining, the children were laughing, I got to lie in bed until about seven. It was lovely. My mom and dad are here for treatment this week. Papa is staying with the boys while Mimi is coming with me to see what The Block Center (I'm calling it "TBC") is all about. Pete will be gone for work then home with Papa and the boys in the evening.

My mom and I were packed up in good time. We ran errands without a hitch. Made fairly good time on the drive to TBC. I told my mom on the way there how strange the drive was. On the one hand, I was nervous about treatment (due to some difficult side effects the first time), and yet how excited I was to be going back to TBC. Checked in, had my port accessed, and was ready to go with Vitamin C by 12:30 p.m.

There is a cooking class four days a week at TBC. We made it just in time to catch the tail end of the demonstration and to enjoy some of the food it had produced. Afterward, I met with the financial personnel who gave me a voucher to stay at an area hotel for one night (we stay two nights).

Back in the treatment pod, I had a talk with the Physician's Assistant, Jen, about some rough side effects I'd had after the last treatment (especially but not limited to the most painful stomach cramps I have ever endured in my life to the point of nearly passing out from the pain...). She made some suggestions and told me to discuss them with Dr. Block later. I agreed to most certainly do that.

My mom and I were able to spend some time talking and I caught her up on the full documentation of the head-shaving event. We had a little time to chat and soak up the sunshine streaming in from the windows beside and above us, when a friend and former supervisor of mine from The Cancer Support Center came to talk with me. She is now working at TBC and it was wonderful to get to see her and catch up a bit.

After our visit, I went to a personalized yoga session, which was A. Mazing! I want that every day. Because of the space issue, my mom was not able to participate, but she watched to see what I was learning. I felt so wonderful after stretching, relaxing, meditating, breathing. A. Mazing.

Feeling good and back in my pod—not the usual Hickory (that was taken by the time we arrived) —we camped out next door at Fir. I finished up the Vitamin C and had the line capped off until tomorrow.

Dr. Block came to meet with us, to end the day. It was so nice to be able to check in with him about the things I had discussed with the PA in regard to the side effects from my first treatment and brainstorming ways to prevent the same from happening this time around. He is a very genuine and pleasant person. Just what I would imagine anyone would want in a doctor. I also appreciate the way he thinks about medicine, and that doesn't always mean conventional medicine. Many of the ideas we came up with for troubleshooting the side effects of last treatment were natural. I was happy that it wasn't more prescriptions. (I have a *box* full of those, y'all! Well, I have a box full of supplements too, but still prefer the natural interventions.) We discussed implications for future treatment due to the diagnosis/discovery of Li-Fraumeni Syndrome. I will know more about that after my appointment with the genetics counselor in a couple of weeks. We also discussed the referrals he had given for surgeons (both home runs), and I thanked him for each. Both surgeons were kind, personable, and took time to talk with me. In such a delicate situation, that was exactly what I (and Pete) needed. I have to say it's easy to trust a referral from a doc you really like, and I told Dr. Block as much.

Make Yourself...

All in all, it had been a fine day. TBC was found to be quite warm due to all of the lovely windows that let in such beautiful sunlight, so when Mom and I were leaving we decided it would be nice to go to the outdoor mall and walk around, maybe do a little window shopping and grab a bite to eat before going to our hotel.

With voucher in hand we went to the hotel and unloaded the car, walked into the impressive lobby, and waited in line for our turn. I was excited at the prospect of staying here even if just for one night. It just looked like such a nice place. Upon reaching the desk, I was promptly told that the hotel was booked for the night. I would be able to use the voucher for the following night, should I choose. I booked the room for the next night and, while a bit put out, was undaunted. Two separate hotels share the parking lot. For tomorrow, we would be able to simply scoot across the parking lot and check in. I entered the lobby of the other hotel and inquired about a room. No room at the inn. Hmm. I was starting to get a bit worried.

For the next twenty minutes, using Yelp and a prayer, I called several different area hotels. All booked. All booked on a Tuesday night. Full house. I could not believe it. Pete called soon after receiving the following text from me: "We can never come here without a reservation again." He suggested that he look on Priceline for a hotel. Within ten minutes, we had a reservation and were checking into the second hotel we had visited.

With a smile on our faces and a collective deep breath, we grabbed our room keys and asked where the best place to park would be to unload the vehicle and head to the room. They directed us around to the side of the building nearest our room. This would have been ideal if, unbeknownst to us, the elevator not been located in the lobby. We parked around

---

94

side the building and walked with our arms loaded down the length of two and a half halls only to find our way back to the lobby to use the elevator. Double-*hmm*.

With room keys in hand, we trekked back down two and a half hallways to get to our assigned room. At the door, I said something to my mom and pointed toward the door. As I spoke, a dog with a deep, gruff voice started barking in the room across the hall. We looked at each other and shook our heads. About-face.

Back down to the lobby to inquire after another room (which I already knew was more than a long shot). While going back and forth with not one, not two, but three different ladies behind the desk it was determined that we could, no wait, we couldn't be changed to another room. We resigned ourselves to our lot and headed up to unpack.

Unpacking, I was looking for the pre- medication I was to take that evening at dinner. It is important for me to take this medication to avoid a reaction to the chemotherapy I would be receiving the next day. The search began patiently searching every bag I packed for myself, twice, thrice then turned into a frantic flurry of dumping bags, rearranging purses, and ended in a call to Pete. Before I had left home my box (yes, *box*) of medications had been flung to the floor in a collision with sweet Sammy. I thought perhaps the medication had rolled under the dresser or chair in the living room. Pete checked into it and that was a negative. So I did what any person in my situation would do; I called the on-call doctor to beg for a prescription. I left a calm but urgent

message with the answering service and awaited their return call. They called moments later and connected me with the on-call doc who interrupted my attempts to explain my situation by yelling, "I can't hear you! I'm in my car and you're on speakerphone. Can you speak up?"
So I yelled back explaining my situation in detail and she very quickly responded, "I can't help you."

What?

"You will have to call your regular doctor and ask him to help you. Call the answering service back and tell them to get in contact with him."
Near tears, I called the answering service back and explained in great detail all that the "on-call" doctor had said to me. The woman I spoke to, with a deep sigh, told me she would make the call.

While waiting for yet another call from yet another doctor, I applied my coping strategies to calm myself down, using the new form of deep breathing I had learned in yoga earlier in the day, telling my body to relax. It was working. I received a call from said doctor who was very clearly frustrated from the word "Hello."
"I don't know how I'm supposed to help you. I don't have your chart in front of me. I'm not at the office. I don't know what medication you need."

In a soothing tone, I explained that I had had the same prescription added to my regime last visit and a Walgreens in

---

the area had filled it. Perhaps they would have record of the exact dosage and could help us. He was agreeable to this idea and instructed me to contact said Walgreens and give them his answering service number. He dictated the number to me and because my pen wouldn't work it took several tries to actually get the number down.

Praise God for Walgreens. I called, gave my name, and inquired about the script. They told me my refill would be ready in an hour! Just like that. Just. Like. That. I called the answering service and left a message for the doctor that the script was being filled and headed off to a previously scheduled outing with my mom—Whole Foods.

Be Happy...

We made our way through some very hefty I- want-to-get-home-after-a-crazy-day-of-work-so-I'm- driving-like-mad traffic between Skokie and Evanston. As we drove, we discussed the events of the evening. I was determined to make sense of it. There *had* to be a lesson in it...just had to be. What was the meaning of it all? My mom and I suggested to one another that perhaps lessons of joy, patience, perseverance, and/or kindness were behind it all.

Thankfully, we made it safely to the Whole Foods Store and no I-don't-ride-in-the-bike-lane- cyclists were harmed in the process. It was a nice relaxing time to walk through the store and stock up on the good foods that we would be snacking on for the next couple of days. For me, I was anxious to find some of the ingredients and supplements that had been suggested to prevent painful side effects. I found all but one thing and knew that could be found elsewhere, so I left feeling encouraged that things were coming together. While in the store perusing, I received a text from Walgreens saying that my prescription was ready. I was happy to see the text but hesitant to celebrate just yet.

Traffic had dissipated since our drive to Whole Foods, making our trip from Whole Foods much less stressful. The evening was cooling off, the sun setting, and I had applied some newly acquired breathing techniques and smiles to help my shoulders drop and loosen. No need to remain tense, I told myself.

Google Maps took us straight to the Skokie Boulevard Walgreens where I purchased pink earplugs, a bag of almonds, and my much-needed prescription, all for under $19. I must say I left with a (genuine) smile on my face. Things were coming together and it seemed as though the perseverance, patience (kind of), and kindness my mother and I were determined to practice in the midst of the mess was paying off.

Happiness is a SkinnyLicious French Country Salad from The Cheesecake Factory with romaine lettuce, grilled asparagus, fresh beets, goat cheese, candied pecans, and vinaigrette at 8:00 p.m. with my mom. It was so refreshing to put food in our stomachs, and our collective frame of mind truly improved with the nourishment. It also helped that that salad was A. Mazing. For the second time today, something was A. Mazing. (I'm sure there were more "A. Mazings" in this day that I may have failed to recognize and will look for more tomorrow!)

"Happiness cannot be traveled to, owned, earned, or worn. It is the spiritual experience of living every minute with love, grace, and gratitude." -Denis Waitley
"...and it is only then that pure joy can truly be experienced." -Sarah Fenlon Falk

"Consider it pure joy, my brothers and sisters, whenever you face trials of many kinds, because you know that the testing of your faith produces perseverance. Let perseverance finish its work so that you may be mature and complete, not lacking anything." James 1:2-4 NIV

4/15/15
Our Bodies are Sacred;
Continued Growth in Care;
and Honoring of Self and Others

Wednesday, 4/15/15, 3:30 a.m.

As I've been learning to regard my body as more than just a vehicle propelling me through life and learning to truly care for myself, my respect for all members of my body has increased. My respect for all members of others' bodies has increased as well. On a spiritual level, I would see others mistreat and misuse themselves in different ways and feel sorrow over the lack of care and concern they had for themselves. I believed I had been caring for myself and perhaps have been all this time on some level, but that level of care is deepening, softening, changing. That care is my primary focus, because if I cannot properly care for myself, I will not know how to properly care for others. I teach self-care in many different forms to my clients in my private practice, to my home care patients, and even my coworkers.

This is a very important process for me to truly learn,

adopt, and live. We exploit and ravage our bodies in so many ways. I recognize it more as I embrace this change into a deepening respect for my body. One way I still struggle to maintain appropriate boundaries with myself is in the area of sleep. Most nights I don't get enough of it. I will do and do and do whatever is in my line of sight that needs doing until it's after 10:00 p.m., and I had told myself to be ready to wind down by 8:00! Not only that, but my mind really turns on at night and I could write and think and write and think until 1:00 a.m. or later—and I do sometimes. Even now, I was awakened at 3:30 a.m. and my mind won't shut off. There were thoughts I needed to get out and so here I am trying to get them out so that I can go back to sleep!

I would encourage anyone to consider ways that they exploit their bodies through food, drink, drugs, lack of sleep, negative thoughts, allowing toxic people in, unlimited stress, inappropriate boundaries (or lack of boundaries altogether), sexual habits, and any other way a person might contrive to misuse their one and only personal, God-given resource. Our bodies are resilient and were created to heal themselves, but they are not infallible or immortal. We must do what we can to nurture and sustain this precious resource. It's vital that we continue to grow in respect and honor of our bodies.

"Do you not know that your bodies are temples of the Holy Spirit whom you received from God? You are not your own, you were bought with a price. Therefore, honor God with your bodies." 1 Corinthians 6:19-20.

Thursday, 4/16/15, 4:45 a.m.

I learned the Cobbler pose in my personalized yoga session on Tuesday and have been utilizing that and the new deep breathing technique I also learned there. In this new form of breathing, I breathe in and out through the nose. This form of breathing directs the airflow through the nostrils, which have a filtering system, but also serves to retain the body's natural moisture. I had always practiced breathing in through the nose and exhaling through the mouth but apparently one loses more moisture in this form of breathing and it's counterproductive if you want to stay well hydrated.

Both Tuesday and Wednesday night, I have begun by assuming the Cobbler pose as I get into bed. This pose serves to open up the lymphatic systems, giving them plenty of space to do their filtering work. I employ the breathing techniques and hold the pose, arms outstretched for a few minutes, all the while guiding my body into peaceful, healing relaxation. I talk to each part of my body, each muscle group, inviting my whole body into this state.

Next, I lay hands on the tumor sites and instruct all of my fighter cells and the chemotherapy (once I've had it) that the battle is here and I visualize all those warriors coming to battle to finish off the cancer. I imagine the cancer casualties being filtered away by my lymphatic system that is lying open and functioning at top form.Then I lay hands on each of my organs and pray for proper function, protection, and healing. I receive God's promises and remember that by the stripes Christ suffered on the cross, I am healed. "But He was pierced for our transgressions, He was crushed for our sins; the punishment that brought us peace was on Him, and by His wounds we are healed." Isaiah 53:5

Once I feel my body in a state of complete relaxation and proper function, I lengthen and strengthen, first stretching my legs out. I point my toes, then flex my feet and stretch my heels. Next, I extend my arms above my head and hold a stretch. I hold this pose for a few minutes and just feel the benefit and the power in it. Then I return to the Cobbler Pose. (I really encourage anyone to look into this pose and to practice it.)

I remain in the Cobbler Pose with my hands on my abdomen to provide support to all my filtering systems that are working harder now since chemotherapy has been introduced to the battle. Then I turn my prayers and healing attention to all those I know who are in need of healing. I pray that God's love and healing, which transcends time, distance, and space, would minister to them. I pray for peace, healing, and joy in the midst of the struggle for all involved. I know well enough that dealing with disease and illness is not one person's effort; it affects all of those who love and care for you.

I pray for joy because I also know how important attitude is in this process. Proverbs 17:22 says, "A cheerful heart is good medicine, but a crushed spirit dries up the bones." I believe it's valuable to pray for the spirit and mindset of each person involved to lift them up! God's light is never brighter than in our darkest hours.

This bedtime practice of honoring my body and assisting in its healing process also reminds me to honor and pray for the healing processes of others. I feel lifted up by the support, prayers, love, and positivity of all of those who text me, call me, message me, comment on Facebook, and send me cards in the mail. I have said it before and I will say it again: I truly feel carried by those thoughts and prayers. It is the hope of my heart to return that strength and support in any way that I can.

4/16/15
Second Day One

Yesterday was a better experience because I wasn't dealing with the after-effects of anesthesia, which had been difficult to recover from during my first treatment after my port-placement surgery. While it is an outpatient surgery and the anesthetics are light, my body doesn't handle them well and so it was a bit of a struggle for a few days.

My mind was sharp yesterday, until the Benadryl, but for the most part sharp! I felt accomplished. I started the day with fifteen minutes on the treadmill That's five more minutes than last treatment. I was able to meet with the financial person to discuss lodging options and possible reduced medical rates for my next treatment stay and, of course, we discussed bills accrued.

Later, my mom and I introduced ourselves around or were introduced to some of the other wellness warriors and families in treatment alongside me. I read, wrote, slept (because I needed some catch-up after my early morning and due to the Benadryl), and chatted with my mom (while awake).

The pharmacy stalled our progress a bit so there was some "unplugged" (no IV line hooked up) downtime where there were no drugs being administered and we had to wait. I didn't mind much due to the fact that I was back in my "Hickory" pod, seated in a comfortable chair with a pile of things I wanted to read or write and all the while, the sun was shining down on me from the windows above.

"Ahh," I thought, *"if one has to be treated for cancer I can't think of a better place to be."*

Treatment was resumed and we finished out our day around six p.m. I felt stronger than I had last go-around and was even able to drive away from The Block Center and spend a little shop time at Target before heading *back* to The Cheesecake Factory for another SkinnyLicious French Country Salad with romaine lettuce, fresh beets, grilled asparagus, candied pecans, goat cheese (an indulgence on my diet) and vinaigrette.

My mom and I were both very tired by the time we reached the hotel but it was a satisfied and accomplished fatigue. I sewed a couple of hats I had found at Target to better fit my bald head, put on my warm stocking cap, took my melatonin, and a drink of water and laid down in the Cobbler Pose to begin my new going-to-bed practices. You can read about them at length in my previous post "Our Bodies are Sacred; Continued Growth in Care; and Honoring of Self and Others."

All in all, I thank God for a smooth and successful second day one, done.

4/17/15
Me, In Context of Time With My Mom

Being with my mom at The Block Center during my treatment created a different dynamic this week. I would say there were other factors that made the experience different in the first place. For instance, I was not recovering from anesthesia this time around. While I was coming in a little weaker than the first treatment, having just started feeling more like myself for maybe four or five days before having to return, I believe I was still in a better place.

It was nice to have my mom there so that she could experience The Block Center as compared to the sometimes/somewhat traumatic memories we share of our time together during my first cancer treatment. We did recall all of the blessings during our time in 1991-92 and all of the amazing people we met on our journey. It seems whenever you are in a dark spot of life, the light of resiliency and hope still shines so brightly. We met many bright and hopeful people that year going through some of the most difficult things I had ever encountered.

At The Block Center this week, my mom introduced herself to many of the people around me. I, being more alert and aware this week, was able to interact as well. It was a pattern and style of interacting that I remembered well from our first days in the hospital in Michigan, learning our way through the hallways, medical-speak, and way of life as full-time cancer patient/caregiver. My mom and I, in those days, had become the nurse instigated/self-designated welcoming committee on the seventh floor at Mott Children's Hospital in Ann Arbor. We provided an unofficial orientation of sorts. We gained many friends that way and worked to encourage others as they began their cancer journey.

That day at The Block Center, in a much different setting than the clinical one where we had spent much time in the past, led by my mom's extroverted introductions, we strolled the hardwood floors and smiled at others sitting in their recliners, stopping to chat when the opportunity arose. It was nice to talk with others and hear their stories, journeys, and struggles. While every experience was so different, there was comfort in knowing we were not alone. I hoped that our story and struggles were in some way comforting to those who listened as well.

Today, as I write this, I realize there is much more to say on this subject but my mind is so sluggish. I've been very tired and somewhat lethargic today. My body is recovering. My mind is trying to keep up.

I remember even on my weakest days in 1991-92, nurses would ask if they could send someone in to talk, or if I would feel up to meeting "the new kid." My mom probably did more than I, spending time and sharing tears with other parents while we the patients slept. I know this: we draw strength from one another. Hearing the testimonies of strength and hope in the midst of pain and suffering encourages me to dig deep and find the fortitude I need to carry on. And in the times I feel I have nothing to give, I know that merely sharing my struggle with another may just be the encouragement they need to find the way through their own challenge.

My Mom and I, both breast cancer survivors,

in September 2015

Photo by Cindy Heimberger. Used with permission.

Letter from my mom, Spring 1992, nearing the end of my treatment for bone cancer:

Dear Daughter,

Remember James Dobson saying something about this "mother/daughter thing" growing up? Well, he wasn't talking about a positive "thing" but believe me there really is a very special "mother/daughter thing" that happens. There's nothing else like it. Some day, God willing, you'll understand.

It says in Colossians 3 that we "can do ALL things through Christ who strengthens us." IF ANYONE CAN, YOU CAN. I love you. I love you. I love you. I'm so very proud of you. XOXO

The Lord bless you and keep you. The Lord make His face shine upon you. The Lord lift up His countenance upon you and give you peace.

Amen!
Love – Mom

5/5/15
Dreams and Promises

I've had two very vivid dreams in the last week. Since I
believe that God can speak to us in a variety of ways,
including dreams, I've been thinking about and praying on
these particular dreams.

In the first dream, I knew there was someone in my life
who had had a baby that they did not think they would be
able to care for and wanted to allow the baby to be adopted. I
had such a deep sense of love for this baby and determination
that this baby would be a part of our family. I was crying in
my dream and stressing that this child was ours. Even though
the details hadn't been worked out, I already knew it would
all come together and the baby already *was* part of our
family.

Birth in the context of a dream can symbolize a number of
things. Of course, many pregnant women do dream about
their babies before birth. I, however, am not pregnant. Birth
can also symbolize something new in life that will cause a

great change. Since I consider life precious and every birth a miracle, I am really excited to have a dream such as this and to see what miracle or wonder is in store! I've been praying to be open to what God would have for me and would be aware of this new work that He is doing in my life. And I pray that Pete, my partner in all of this life, would also have eyes to see where God is leading and what He is doing in our life and family.

There have been no clear changes as of this moment. But there is *a lot* going on in our family right now and this dream of birth has at the very least increased the measure of hope I hold in my heart. It led me to revisit the Scripture that was my theme verse during my first experience with cancer in 1991-92.

"'For I know the plans I have for you,' declares the Lord. 'Plans to prosper you and not to harm you. Plans for hope and a future.'" Jeremiah 29:11

The second vivid dream I had this week has truly touched me to the core. I'd like to give a little backstory before sharing this dream. In one of my previous posts, "Growing Gracefully and Knowledge of the Mutated Gene," I explained results from one of the genetic tests I've taken since being diagnosed with my second primary cancer in twenty-two years. I tested positive for Li-Fraumeni, a genetic syndrome that has to do with a mutated tumor suppressor gene. I am still learning more about it and would encourage you to Google it should you be interested in learning more. The long and short of Li-Fraumeni is that my risk for developing certain types of cancer is higher than the average person's, sometimes substantially higher. Since learning of this mutated gene, it has been an emotional and intellectual roller coaster for me. I've told myself, "This is simply information that will inform the future of my medical treatment and care." Intellectually, that makes sense and is true. Emotionally, I've felt as if I'll be chasing my proverbial tail (cancer) for the rest of my life! And since it is genetic, there's a 50/50 chance each of my children may carry the gene and I can't even begin to imagine what that will mean for my family and the future of each of my children. I'm so grateful for my faith that reminds me that I do not hold the future, but I know Who does! Faith does not call for certainty; it calls for hope and trust. It calls for moving forward, one step at a time, regardless of whether or not the next foothold is in view.

This next dream of mine I'm still praying on, but let me say that I get chills every time I recount it. In my dream, I was driving a car (not my mommy mini-van!) and it seemed to be indoors for some reason, but there was a sidewalk beside the road. I passed an orange (my favorite color) tricycle on the sidewalk. I noticed it but didn't think much of it. Then moments later, I saw it again farther down the road. At that point, someone said to me, "Sarah, would you look!" Obediently, I stopped the car, got out, and was looking more closely at the tricycle. The voice urged again, "Sarah, look!" When I looked up, I saw a vehicle farther on past the tricycle. It was a black vehicle and I instinctively looked into the back seat. On a leather seat I saw a pretty, elderly lady sitting there and when she saw me she smiled and said, "Sarah, do you understand? Do you know who I am?" Immediately I began to cry (in my dream and in reality) and nodded my head. "Yes, I understand," I replied. I knew in that instant that the old woman was me!

Since being diagnosed with breast cancer in February I've not asked God for reassurance that I will be here to watch my boys grow up or to celebrate a silver anniversary. While I understand the gravity of this cancer diagnosis, I have tried not to look too far ahead, as that can be greatly overwhelming. I'm simply hoping to get good sleep tonight; I don't have the energy to worry about what tomorrow will bring.

I am learning to have more faith for myself but also more faith for others when I pray on their behalf, impatient to see my expectations met. In my heart, it is clear that healing does not always come on this side of heaven. Answers are not always given here on earth. Sometimes God wants us to wait and talk to Him about it in person. So, whether these dreams are direct messages from the God whom I trust or merely thoughts for me to ponder, I choose to put my hope in Him and continue to praise him. I will keep my eyes on Him and will not be shaken. I read this today and it blew me away. I pray this brings encouragement and hope, a refill of faith, to all who read it:

Psalm 16:5-11 NIV: "Lord, you alone are my portion and my cup; You make my lot secure. The boundary lines have fallen for me in pleasant places; surely I have a delightful inheritance. I will praise the Lord, who counsels me; even at night my heart instructs me. I keep my eyes always on the Lord. With Him at my right hand, I will not be shaken. Therefore my heart is glad and my tongue rejoices; my body also will rest secure, because you will not abandon me to the realm of the dead, nor will you let your faithful one see decay. You make known to me the path of life; You will fill me with joy in your presence, with eternal pleasures at your right hand."

5/7/15
Stability and Another Day One Done

The last two weeks have been among the most emotional that
I've spent in some time. I was crying about everything and
anything, but at the core is this deep grief over the loss of
health, strength, energy, and stability. In times such as these,
the stability of family life is impacted, the stability of self,
the stability of faith, all of these are tested.

I posted on Facebook that I was having a very difficult
time preparing emotionally and mentally for this round of
chemo. In each of my previous two treatments, there have
been rough rebounds and just when I'm feeling more like
myself, I find it's time to turn around and do it again. It's a
crazy carnival ride! This round and round was truly testing
the stability of self. Could I make myself keep this up? I
joked with Pete that he would have to tranquilize me and
carry me in for chemo. (I was only half joking at the time.)

During the last treatment, my parents came to watch the
fellas at home, and then took them on a road trip to visit their
cousins in New Jersey. So I didn't see my babies for one

week and three days. While I was in bed, weak, couldn't even *see* the housework that needed to be done and went back to work half days so I could go back to bed all afternoon, I still missed those children like mad. I could see the absolute impact on the stability of family life that this illness and subsequent treatment invokes.

In some ways I was glad the boys didn't have to be there with me in bed all the time telling them to "go play" or "let's watch (another) movie" because that's all I could have mustered those first couple weeks after treatment. They had a blast with their Mimi and Papa and getting to go to see Lillian, Maggie, Uncle Jake, and Aunt Jeannine. The joy those little boys bring to me cannot be measured and the healing produced in the midst of that joy and love is boundless! I was so happy to have them home at the end of it! And I was starting to feel better, so that served to improve the time we would have together until the next treatment.

I worked on Monday and struggled. I didn't struggle with work but with focus and clarity. It was like my lifeline, the one strung between my heart and the heart of the Creator God, our heavenly Father, the Great Physician, was washed over by a wave of confusion and doubt. The lifeline was all jammed up! I was in the midst of a crisis of faith and I knew it. But God provides. He speaks to us out of the darkness, through the chaos. He speaks in dreams, in nature, in Scripture, and in the voice of a friend. During part of my work day, I was having computer issues, as we sometimes do in our workdays, and this required a meeting with someone I knew would not only assist me with my computer issues but someone I could talk to about my stability of faith issues too.

I've been known to say that "Faith does not call for certainty, it calls for hope and trust. It calls for moving forward, one step at a time, regardless of whether or not the next foothold is in view." So I know that a faith crisis simply serves to deepen our faith through struggle and determination, resulting in a peace that no one can understand because it is simply divine. I was not afraid of this faith crisis, but I knew I needed to seek wise counsel in the midst of it. Shannel had provided me with a shot-in-the-arm, faith-filler conversation at another point in my life when I needed it and here she was, on my schedule due to computer issues and I knew it was a Divine appointment that day.

Shannel reminded me to be open to God, to pray that whatever I might be thinking or feeling would not block the blessing that God had in store for me. I applied that truth to the jammed-up lifeline too. I didn't want my fears and frustrations to block my path to God. I wanted fear and frustrations to simply serve as reminders to look for grace and that Divine, unimaginable peace in the midst of them. My friend reminded me that our view is so limited but God sees the big picture (how many times will God have to send friends into my path to remind me of this!). I shared my dreams with Shannel and began to recount God's faithfulness and provision in my life. It was such a nice conversation of hope, healing, and praise even in the midst of my faith crisis and Shannel's most recent loss of a loved one. We know our heavenly Father is caring for us. I left with computer issues resolved and my spirit uplifted and encouraged.

Tuesday we had a bit of a rocky start. We didn't get out the door when we anticipated and the departure wasn't a smooth one with four boys wanting to go in four different directions. I knew I was in for it when, between our house in Kankakee, where it was sunny and a balmy 70°-something and the eleven miles to Cindy's house where the kids would be dropped off and staying for a few days, the temperature dropped about 15° (and kept falling) with a steady rain. I had left my new spring jacket, yes rain-resistant, on my bed because the weather report had said 70-80-some degrees for the next few days, so I packed accordingly! I had based this on a weather report for Kankakee. By the time we had said our good-byes (with tears shed by me), I had borrowed a raincoat from Cindy, and we had driven another twenty miles north, the temperature was still dropping. It dropped to 57° by the time we reached The Block Center. I was wearing sandals, linen pants, and a short-sleeve tee. I was the picture of summertime. Doctor Penny Block even made mention of my attire—"looks like you're ready for spring"—when she first saw me. I wanted to borrow her overcoat! I cried tears over my new coat that would have worked perfectly in such a time and temp as this. Of course, those tears were not for the coat. Here I was, about to "do it again." This crazy carnival ride that just didn't make sense, here I was hopping on for another go. So, I posted on Facebook "Prayer support appreciated" and I must say, I could feel the prayers. I know there are many friends and family who are praying for me, and I have said it before that I feel lifted by those prayers. It is true, always true. I am so very grateful for those who pray, send cards of encouragement, share Scriptures, and love and hope with me.

Today, another Day One, done. It was a good day. I was able to catch up briefly with a couple I'd met last time through my mom. They asked about her and we talked a bit. It was nice to have more familiar faces to see. My nurse Jessica is just amazing anyway, but she always brings a smile, shares part of herself with me, and makes me laugh. I think we have similar senses of humor. It's just nice. God chose the perfect nurse for me! The PA, Jen, who is as cute as a button both in looks and personality, was such an encouragement for me today.

I had a breast exam for the first time since starting chemo and Jen confirmed what I already knew: the tumor has shrunk so much it is no longer palpable; neither is the one lymph node that could be felt at one time. Such good news! The treatment and the prayers are working! Another thing discovered during my exam was that I have a hernia. I had my suspicions ever since having William twenty months ago! I had been having trouble breathing at times when trying to lift things, so I was wearing the fancy little belly support bands that they give you after a C- section and using it to support my abdomen where I was feeling the strain. Jen told me that was a really smart thing for me to do. (I didn't know I was being smart, I just knew it felt better if I wore it!) So she expressed that the type of reconstruction I'm considering for my surgery later this year (more on that later) would probably help to fix that, along with learning more yoga/Pilates to strengthen those abdominal muscles that have been compromised. I felt so validated and encouraged after that exam!

My thoughtful, helpful friend Cindy *knew* pictures of my kids would be just the things to cheer me, and so she sent pictures of their adventures throughout the day. Each one made me smile. It's also such a blessing to know how well my kiddos are being looked after while we are here and they are there.

The next bit of encouragement I was to receive throughout the day was this post on Facebook, coming from a mama who is going through some kind of struggle I can't even imagine: "This is my command—be strong and courageous! Do not be afraid or discouraged. For the Lord your God is with you wherever you go." Joshua 1:9. This is their family's verse during a difficult time of seeking the health and healing of their young son. She shared it in hopes of encouraging others. It encouraged me today.

There have been so many who have left cards for me to find at my house and words of encouragement on Facebook, or sent cards, or provided meals, all to show care, concern, and support. It is acknowledged and appreciated more than words can express. And speaking of more than words can express...

My husband has been such an encouragement to me since this all started. Pete is/has been a cheerleader, a coach, a patient partner, and hard worker both at home and in his career. He shared this prayer with me at the beginning of our day. It is entitled "Let Your Healing Light Shine" from Richard Foster's book, *Prayers from the Heart:* "Let Your healing light shine, O God.Give doctors unusual skill in the healing arts. Give researchers success in curing diseases. Give counselors insight and healing love. Give pastors discernment and tender compassion. Give social workers courage and boundless love. Let Your healing light shine, O God. Amen."

I go to bed (finally!) with a heart that feels stable. I have received my "daily bread" as we ask for it in The Lord's Prayer. And tomorrow I will need to make that request again. But for now, I'm thankful that another day one is officially done.

5/13/15
Life in Paradox

I've started noticing the pink bumper stickers around town, the ones that are in bold print, sometimes sporting a pair of boxing gloves and proudly instruct, "FIGHT LIKE A GIRL." When this symbol and phrase first caught my attention, I was totally into it. I thought, *"That's right!"* Cancer is tough business no matter how you choose to address it. While I didn't have catchphrases and logos the first time I was diagnosed with cancer, and never even knew the color of the ribbon for osteogenic sarcoma until a few years ago (it's gold), I spent so much time at the hospital and with others of like age and diagnosis that I had a strong sense of community.

I've not been a ribbon-wearing member of any group but I do understand the comfort and strength drawn from identifying with a community. However, the more I think about the "fight" part of it, the more uneasy I have become. In regards to the way I have chosen to approach this diagnosis and treatment, "fight" seems too combative. I would rather float.

Imagine this: it's a warm summer day. Looking out in front of you, you see the sun's rays reflecting off the surface of a beautiful, clear, flowing river, shining like diamonds on the water. You lift your face toward the sky. Eyes close gently. And you feel the warmth of the sun upon you. The gentle breeze that blows keeps your temperature even and comfortable. It's the perfect day. The birds are singing their songs of praise. The gentle lapping of the water matches the rhythm of your heartbeat. The scent of flowers in full bloom fills your mind with magnificent colors and images. You breathe deeply and as you do, you find yourself floating. You are floating on the surface of the water and yet you do not get wet. It is some miracle that carries you, effortlessly, freely, softly onward. You float on your gentle way while in complete relaxation, complete peace, rest.

That is the place my mind takes me when I think too hard on fighting. It's almost like, I can't. Not that I give up. I don't give up. I keep going. Not in a forceful way, but in a gentle way. It must be gentle or I can't. I know some people get pumped up with the call to fight and I even have my moments when I feel a sense of pride at the color pink or when thinking about how tough a person has to be to deal with an illness or disability and to thrive within it.

Often, lately, people have been telling me how strong I am, how tough. All I can say is, I don't feel like it at all. I feel weak, vulnerable, and sad. In the same respect, I feel hopeful and resilient; I am filled with gratitude for all of the blessings in my life. It's a wonderful life. I have a husband the likes of whom I never would have thought to ask for myself; four beautiful boys who are healthy, happy, smart, and loving; healthy, present parents; a friend who would do anything for us at anytime; a sweet little house; a dependable vehicle; a career I enjoy; a wonderful community to live in; food in the refrigerator and so much more...

I'm learning it's okay to live in a constant state of paradox: weak, vulnerable, sad, hopeful, resilient, grateful, blessed. I'm a warrior princess but in the most calm and gentle sense of it. I keep going and don't stop. I'll do whatever it takes, but I can't think of it as fighting, I must think of it as floating.

I've been so emotional of late, easily overwhelmed. I've taken to reading very short devotionals, bite-size pieces of encouragement. Sometimes I have to read the same one a few days in a row because my mind and heart can't hold the full truth of it the first go-round. So it was with the entry I will share here. I read it after being home for a couple days after this last treatment. Feeling totally depleted physically, emotionally, and spiritually, these words from the book *Everyday Prayers & Praises* lifted me: "Hope and Healing- My health may fail, and my spirit may grow weak, but God remains the strength of my heart; He is mine forever. Psalm 73:26 NLT"

Your body is amazingly resilient, yet terminally fragile. Fashioned by God's lovingly creative hand, it was not designed to last. But you were. That's because you are so much more than your body. Even if your health fails, He will not. He is near. He hears every prayer, even those you hesitate to pray. Call on Him. His hope and healing reach beyond this life into the next.

Amazingly resilient yet terminally fragile, sad yet hopeful: life in paradox. I'll continue gently on and won't stop. I won't stop. I'll fight like a girl and float.

5/18/15
Inner Monologue, Madness, and Staying the Course

I have been in a dark place the past couple of days. It's been very difficult to eat. Not because of nausea, thank God, but rather because my taste buds are so fried that food tastes like ash or grit in my mouth. I can take a couple bites of food and then I gag. The rub is that everything smells, looks, and sounds great but then it enters my mouth and...*bleck*. It is causing a significant amount of mental and emotional anguish. I've bawled my eyes out on numerous occasions, tears flooding past my almost bald eyelids, throat sore and tight. "I can't eat," I squeak pathetically. This happens about every mealtime. It's so depressing to wake up in the morning with a growling stomach and then to realize that there is close to nothing that will pass this mouth without threatening to send me running to the bathroom.

After working last week amidst this minor crisis, I came home Thursday night with a very sore throat, aches, and chills. By Saturday afternoon I was in the emergency room with a fever of 101.8° and all of the aforementioned symptoms. They ran the works on me: complete blood count (CBC), urinalysis, EKG, and immediately wanted to take me in for a chest X-ray. I refused this initially due to my diagnosis of Li-Fraumeni, a mutated tumor suppressor gene that predisposes me to certain cancers. (In my post "Growing Gracefully and Knowledge of the Mutated Gene," I explain this in more detail.) With Li-Fraumeni, it is often best to avoid exposure to radiation. They said because I was complaining of flank pain, they would wait to see if the infection causing this fever was urinary or kidney- related and then a chest X-ray would be unnecessary. When the urinalysis came back clear, they were very concerned that I had a touch of pneumonia or bronchitis and were insistent that I go ahead with the X-ray. So I did. After a few hours of very excellent care at the hands of the staff in the emergency room at Presence St. Mary's Hospital I was sent home. I had received half a liter of fluid as well as a dose of IV antibiotics while in the ER and was given more antibiotics to take for the upper respiratory infection they detected on my chest X-ray. On the seventh day, I rested.

Last night I slept for about an hour. As I lay there, I wondered how I would survive the next two months on what little food I can get down. Then I allowed myself to think ahead to a massive surgery that is also in my future. I realized I was heading down a dark path and chose to turn my attention to the present in attempt to shrink things down to size. I'm not sure it worked.

I asked myself, "How do you feel?" The first question I actually answered was, "How do I feel *physically*?"

My skin feels thin, as if a layer has been shed. My eyelids hurt if touched; my fingertips are all smooth (my iPhone doesn't recognize my index print anymore); my tongue, throat, and esophagus feel as if there is something growing in them which causes weird sensations and pain; and the inside of my nose also feels as if a protective layer has been removed. I have persistent earaches. My digestive system lets me know where any amount of food, liquid, or air is at all times. My joints ache. I'm hungry. My system is overwhelmed. I'm exhausted.

Then the question, "How do I feel emotionally?" And I began contriving ways to tell my husband, friends, family, and doctor that I was done with chemotherapy because this "crazy carnival ride" of being sick or just not-sick-enough to *not* get more chemo is driving me mad. I was writhing under the weight of the question.

"Silly me," I interrupted. "Silly me" is something we say to each other in our family when we've done something funny, foolish, or absentminded. We don't use the word "stupid."

Silly me. While we were tucking our children in to bed just hours before this inner monologue began, we recited Psalm 23. Our four-year-olds have it memorized. This Psalm holds a few lines that are particularly prudent at this juncture: "The Lord is my Shepherd. I shall not want. He makes me to lie down in green pastures. He leads me beside still waters. He restores my soul...even though I walk through the valley of the shadow of death I will fear no evil for you are with me."

It wasn't until today, the day after the sleepless night full of inner monologues and madness, that I was really able to see things differently. Not until after I started to pitch my plan to quit treatment to my friend Cindy, who probably thought I was mad but was kind enough not to come right out and say so. Cindy took my three older boys for a walk while my little guy slept. This gave me time for myself, time to read, time to think. I called my mom to clue her in on my thoughts and plans. She reminded me to "follow the peace" which has been a theme throughout her approach to addressing her breast cancer diagnosis. She encouraged me to look for God's promises.

I read a post from a blog that I follow. Lisa-Jo Baker posted about buying their first house. What does buying a house have to do with seeing things clearly regarding cancer treatment? Well, Lisa-Jo talked about her deep desire to be in a home of her own for the first time ever, with her husband of fifteen years and three children. It was when she shared about being at the point of "giving up" on her dream that it hit me... Quoting directly from Lisa-Jo's blog, these words spoke straight to my heart: "And more than that, I deeply needed to believe that this answer was from God and not from the whims of the universe. I needed to believe that when we pray and we trust God with our hopes and we ask Him to protect us from the decisions we don't know enough to avoid, that He answers us because He is a good God. And I believe this.

And I needed to believe the No was a loving act from Him and not just a matter of, 'Well, that's life.' Because what is all this faith we talk about worth if in the moments of our greatest hurts or hopes it doesn't count?"

This caused me to remember that when treatment plans were first created, I felt God's peace and presence. I felt that He had led me to The Block Center and to those I would entrust with my care. Even then, I wasn't happy or excited about the prospect of chemotherapy. But this treatment, this cancer journey, this life isn't about being happy, excited, or even comfortable. And since it isn't about all that, it makes this promise that came to my mind this afternoon all the more meaningful: [Jesus said,] "Very truly I tell you, you will weep and mourn... You will grieve but your grief will turn to joy. ...I have told you these things, so that in me you may have peace. In this world you will have trouble. But take heart! I have overcome the world!" John 16:20, 33

And so, I take heart. I will stay the course. And I do have peace. Thank you, Cindy, for reminding me that I can't just "give up." Thank you, Mom, for reminding me to look back at the promises I've received in the past and to listen closely for new promises. And thank you, Lisa-Jo, for posing the question, "What is all this faith we talk about worth if in the moments of our greatest hurts or hopes it doesn't count?" It made all the difference for me today, ladies.

6/3/15
All About the Boys

I've had a lot of questions lately about the boys. How are the boys doing? How are they handling this cancer treatment-craziness? The truth is: they're amazing. They. Are. Amazing. Each one has his way of caring for his mom and showing his love for me daily.

Bobby, the oldest at five years, seeks to help in whatever way he can and beams with pride when his efforts are acknowledged. Before my diagnosis, I felt he was entering a stage where he was gravitating more toward his dad and guy time, but lately he has stayed close to mom and loves to snuggle more than usual. He asks what would make me feel better, and I know he'd go to the ends of the earth to get it for me. I often respond, "Your hugs." Or simply, "You do!"

Teddy, second oldest son and elder of the four-year-old twins by a minute, brings me flowers from the yard, stickers, and fruit. He asks me when I'll be done with my medicine. I explain that my medicine will be done in July but then I will have to have surgery in August. Ted tries to surround his mom with beautiful things and is so pleased when I display his offerings. The other day he took me by the hand to lead me (with my eyes closed per instructions) to this plant that had bloomed in our flowerbed. He was sharing a beautiful surprise with me and asked that I take a picture.

Sam, our second four-year-old and third son, also offers gifts such as stickers off of his morning banana (every morning he brings it to me, without fail). But his favorite thing to do is to connect with me in regard to our similarities. He reminds me often that we share a favorite color (orange) and like the same foods (when I am actually able to eat). Whatever the case may be, he makes sure to point out where he and I meet and always ends with a hug and a smile. He asks me often when I'm going to feel better. I simply respond, "Soon, buddy. I hope very soon."

William is "the baby" and while he is twenty- one months old, he is still my baby. Will, or Mr. Mister as we all call him, seems to be holding onto everyone more. He will go down the line to find out where everyone is at all times; this includes Cindy, Mimi, Papa and even Molly (our dog) and Maddy (Cindy's dog). This may be natural for his age but it seems noteworthy. With my "disappearance" for a few days every three weeks and the break in structure that creates, I believe he's trying to keep everything and everyone in place in that mind of his. It's always fun when we reunite to have him run into my arms shouting joyfully, "*Mommy!*"

These boys are beautiful, rambunctious, silly, and smart. They continue to learn, grow, and change at lightning speed.

And as I strive to keep up in the midst of work, chores, and treatment, maybe the more appropriate question is: How am I handling them in the midst of this cancer treatment craziness? For their sakes, this is an important question. I'm exhausted and I feel taxed and spent most days from the word go. I often end the day disappointed with myself at my impatience or the way I dealt with things. I strategize how I can avoid those same pitfalls tomorrow. Sometimes it works. Other times, not. But I believe the biggest lesson I've learned is to let go and love. If that's all I do during the day, then it was a great day. I'll let go of those things that would typically weigh me down (the "to- do's"); let go of the way I think my boys should behave (e.g., quieter, calmer, etc.). And I will love every moment. I will love the way they jump around and wrestle one another. I'll love the way their lips quiver when they are put in time out for hitting. I will love the relentless questions and requests at bedtime. I will love the sweaty, sleepy head on my shoulder.

I will have grace for them and for myself. They are gracious with me. I try to be humble and honest with them. I know when I blow it and am sure to apologize to them for "throwing a fit" (indeed that is often the case). I try to limit expectations or plans for the day. The goal is to spend time with my boys and to be present. If there is a chore that is in dire need of completion I will involve all of the boys in the project. They love to help.

I will savor every hug, back rub, hand pat, kiss, flower, sticker, smile, and look from these boys because I know in those, they are loving me. At the end of the day, it is this exchange of love in word and deed that matters.

I could go on and on about my boys. How are they, you ask? They are amazing: very loving and caring toward their mama; I am beyond blessed by them.

Photograph courtesy of their Aunt Cindy.
Used with permission.

6/10/15
Something as Simple as Food

I have been struggling lately. It's not a new issue, but it has gotten worse as treatments have worn on. I can't eat. Or, I can eat but I have to force myself for the most part. Food tastes horrible. The chemotherapy has messed up my taste buds and taints the flavor of almost any food I try to eat, and I try many different things in hope of finding something that will agree with me.

Those closest to me know what a mental challenge this is. It actually causes mental anguish, I would say, at times. Most everything sounds good, looks good, and smells good. The other day I was craving pizza so much. I had thought about it all day. My husband suggested that we order a pizza so I could just give it a try. When the pizza arrived I smelled it, looked at it then just put my hands on the box and sobbed.

"I just want it to taste right," I cried, "I just want it to be good."

It wasn't good. But I was able to eat about five bites before my gag reflex kicked in to remind me that I wasn't in total control. I really think that was a turning point for me, a point when I realized or decided that this just wasn't right. How can it be a good thing for a person to be unable to help herself in the most basic way, by eating? It has been some time since I've had a fully nourishing meal. Drinking protein shakes, which include my supplements, only take me so far. My stomach feels hungry most of the time and I am unable to feed it.

Yesterday showed some improvement. Today was even better. I know each day will be better than the last. In the meantime, I've been losing weight. With so little fat and so little nourishment, I wonder how much of my supplements are even being absorbed in my system.

I just finished listening to the book *Radical Remission* on audiobook and loved it. I would recommend it to anyone and everyone for the sake of their health, wellbeing, and balance. It was such an encouraging piece of work for me to read/hear during such a difficult time. The book provides testimonies of many different cancer survivors and their healing journeys. Some went through traditional cancer treatment; others found healing by other means. The author, Dr. Kelly Turner, outlines the nine things each cancer survivor she interviewed or who shared their story on her website www.radicalremission.com had in common. They are: Radically Changing Your Diet, Taking Control of Your Health, Following Your Intuition, Using Herbs and Supplements, Releasing Suppressed Emotions, Increasing Positive Emotions, Embracing Social Supports, Deepening

Spiritual Connection, Having Strong Reasons for Living.
Before chemo started in March, I had already radically
changed my diet. I was eating a mostly vegan diet with the
occasional exception. I had seen the benefits of this in my
energy level and moderate weight loss. It felt good to know I
was doing something healthy for my body. Since being on
chemo, I have been unable to follow that diet due to my taste
buds changing and the gag reflex. What little I can eat has
been off plan. At this point, however, the goal is simply to
eat.

Another step I had already taken toward health and
balance was the use of supplements. The Block Center
increased the number of supplements I take when I began
treatment. That has been a difficult thing for me to maintain
as well, due to the gag reflex. As many of my supplements as
possible were changed to capsules so I could pour the powder
out of the capsule into my protein shake, since it has been
very difficult for me to take pills lately.

I believe we all have to continue to work for emotional
wellness. The decision to release suppressed emotions and
increase the positive is a daily one. I am not one to suppress
emotions and feel I am able to release those things that need
to get out.

My social support network has been *amazing* from the
first day. I'm often overwhelmed by the love and kindness of
the people at my church, those I work with, friends, family,
and even strangers. I am not averse to speaking up when I
need something. I know there is a blessing in giving as well

as receiving and I feel truly blessed. I tell people I feel carried by the prayers of those who are faithfully praying for me. It's tangible and I'm amazed by it. I know my social support system is an important part of my healing.

I have always had a deep faith. I can see how each step of this life leads me to learn more and grow more. Every situation builds on my faith and my relationship with God. It's this connection that fuels me.

Having Strong Reasons for Living...their names are Bobby, Teddy, Sam, William, and Pete: my loves and my life.

Taking Control of Your Health and Following Your Intuition were very important chapters for me. I said earlier that crying over that box of pizza was a turning point for me. In that moment, I realized how desperate I had become and how out of control I truly felt. Those two important chapters provided such a level of encouragement for me in the midst of deep frustration and sadness. They empowered me by reminding me that I have a voice and the inner sense (intuition) as to how best to care for myself.

Starting with a lack of food and ending with page 290 of *Radical Remission*, I have been on quite a journey of desperation and self-discovery that I will share more about in time. For now, I will say that I feel I am healing from the inside out.

I was reminded tonight in 2 Corinthians 5:17, "Therefore if anyone is in Christ the new creation has come, the old has gone..." Every issue in my life is in Christ because I am. This is good news, as I certainly cannot handle this latest challenge on my own! So I will continue to seek Him in the midst of this situation. I will ask for His wisdom and guidance in this healing process, and choose to believe that very soon I will be able to enjoy even something as simple as food.

6/25/15
Thoughts on Being

Before being diagnosed with cancer the second time, I found that my life was very overwhelming. Being the wife/mom in a family of six places a lot of demands on time and energy. Beyond that, I also realized that I was putting a lot of demands on myself. I had very high, often unrealistic expectations of myself to "do it all" and to always be "better." One can only keep a perfectionist pace for so long before the mind, body, spirit, or all of the above begin to whisper messages such as: "slow it down" or "take care of me." If you don't listen to the whispers, then there will be consequences.

Somewhere along the way, I did hear the whispers, but wasn't sure about how to heed them. In June of last year, I started working with an amazing nutritionist in my area, Kelli Bonomo. I knew that for the sake of my blood sugar levels (I was diagnosed with diabetes in 2001 and had never worked with a nutritionist) and my body's wellbeing that this was a very important step. Working with Kelli for over six months really helped me to learn to balance what was on my plate, to fuel my body effectively, and to care of it with food.

Through conversations with Kelli and in personal quiet time that I was learning to carve out for myself, I began to realize and contemplate other areas of my life that required attention, such as the pressure I was putting on myself, and what that was doing to my emotional and spiritual self. During this time of reflection, I realized how caught up I was with "doing" and rarely let myself simply "be." It was at that point I began to allow myself to be, letting go of the expectations for doing.

The following is the result of this personal discovery:

BE

Grateful: What am I thankful for?

Active: What is my favorite form of movement?

Creative: How do I express myself most positively?

Well-fed: What are my favorite healthy foods?

Positive: What are my strengths?

Spiritual: How do I pray, meditate?

Restful: How is my quiet time and sleep?

Supportive: Gifts are for giving-what gifts do I have to give?

I asked myself these questions over the course of time to consider where I was at with each area of my life. In acknowledging my state of being, I was able to allow what was true about me to come forward. I didn't have to strive or struggle to change, be better or do more, I simply had to *be*; to be genuine and true to who I already was. I also realized that while there are external demands that others would put upon me, coupled with those I put upon myself, the truth of that matter was that giving is an organic part of being as well. We are each gifted in unique ways. So I realized if I allowed myself to be who I was designed to be, then giving of myself (in the ways that only I can) is simply a natural expression of my being.

This paradigm shift was an amazing part of my growth in the last year. I revisit it now in the midst of a situation that could be a war/struggle/fight if I chose to approach it that way. But as I've said before, I choose to float, not fight, with this cancer. I choose to *be*.

6/26/15
The Other Side of Struggle
(Not Beyond It)

I'm done with chemo. The oncologist and I spoke before my last treatment and due to my somewhat extreme and adverse side effects he reduced my dose by 50% total last week. He said if the side effects were the same, though he was convinced I wouldn't feel them at all this time, then I would just be done. The side effects were the same, and I even had a side effect that had disappeared return. I am done with chemo.

It has been a bit anticlimactic, I must admit. There is a sense that something is still hanging over my head. The plan at this point is to continue with Herceptin (a Her2 blocker drug) once every three weeks for the next year. This will be done through IV at The Block Center. I want to go there so I can also receive my IV Vitamin C. The problem with this plan, however, is the condition of my heart. I had an echo done before my last treatment and found that my ejection fraction was diminished by 20%. Ejection fraction is the measurement of how much blood the left ventricle of the heart is pumping with each contraction. A normal ejection fraction is somewhere between 55 and 70. Mine is 40. I looked that up on the American Heart Association website. It says, and I quote, "An ejection fraction between 40 and 55 indicates damage, perhaps from a previous heart attack, but it may not indicate heart failure." *May not* indicate heart failure. Oh good. The decrease in my heart function is attributed to the Herceptin. I was not given Herceptin at my last treatment due to the results of this echo. The doctors I spoke with seemed confident that withholding this dose will allow my heart to "bounce back" and they expected to see an improvement in my ejection fraction next week when I have the echo repeated.

Of course I am concerned for my heart, which has already taken on a lot of hard-hitting drugs in its day. I had a lifetime dose of a chemotherapy drug called Adriamycin in 1991-92, which is also known to damage heart function and was found to indeed have damaged mine.

Going forward, I still have some very weighty decisions to make. I am concerned about the health and function of my heart. I also want to be sure I am doing what is necessary to deal with the cancer that is Her2 positive, the only reason I would be taking Herceptin in the first place.

I went to a gentle yoga class on Wednesday morning. I've wanted to go, and since the boys are with their Mimi and Papa, I took advantage of the opportunity. It was a quiet, soft, slow-paced class. Perfect for my needs. Throughout our time together, we practiced ujjayi (a form of deep breathing, in and out of the nose). I teach deep breathing to my clients and use a different style, breathing in through the nose and exhaling through the mouth. I found ujjayi to be very challenging. I kept wanting to open my mouth, especially since with the exhale, as we were instructed to make a soft noise that only we could hear. With each exhale, I was working to keep my mouth shut and also to coordinate making a noise at the same time. Well, the noise in my ears sounded like panting or choking, or at least something very uncomfortable. I was struggling. Then the instructor said, "The only rule is not to struggle. No struggling here. Just do what you are able."

I felt freed, released to not breathe right if that's what I was doing. With the next exhale, the sound in my head was no longer a choke but instead like a gentle whisper or soft breeze. My pauses in between each breath were not forced or held tightly, they were simple and gentle pauses. This deep breathing practice that I've taught for years took on new life and meaning for me in that moment.

Since then, I have reflected on the transition and recognized that once I let go of struggling, once I set myself free from the expectations of doing it "right," I easily entered into a relaxed state where that style of breathing seemed natural to me. This led me to wonder more about the concept of struggle and to consider what else I might keep myself from.

I listened to an interview with Mary O'Malley, author of the book *What's in the Way IS the Way*. I haven't read the book yet, but I enjoyed the interview and her gentle perspective on life. She talked about the fact that there will always be struggle. Life is like the yin/yang, a dance of light and dark. But if we incorporate and include all of our experiences in life and stop trying to "rid" ourselves of what is uncomfortable or undesirable, then we move toward healing.

Graham Cooke, a Vineyard pastor from the UK, has a two-part YouTube series called "The Art of Thinking Brilliantly" in which he also addresses adversity, trial, and struggle in life. He poses these questions: "What if every trial we face is meant to advance us, to grow us? What if struggle is meant to bring us closer to and make us more aware of the goodness of God?"

As I considered all that I had been experiencing and posed these questions to myself, I came to this conclusion: to me, there is another side to struggle that has nothing to do with discomfort or pain. To me, the other side of struggle *is* the goodness of God, the light in the dark, wisdom gained in the midst of chaos or adversity. So while I face more difficult decisions, I rest in the fact that I am not confronting a foe, but instead I am approaching the Throne of Grace and ultimate Goodness. I am not entering a battle, but am dancing in the light. I can rest in the fact that no matter the circumstance, I will grow here.

7/1/15
More Than Sufficient

Let nothing disturb thee
Let nothing dismay thee
All things pass
God never changes
Patience attains
All it strives for (S)he who has God
Lacks nothing
God alone suffices.

-St. Teresa of Avila

I love this prayer. I think it's beautiful. That last word, however, leaves me feeling unsatisfied every time because this God, my God, *more* than suffices. "Suffice" by definition means to meet or satisfy a need; to be competent or capable. I find the word "lavish," meaning to give in great amounts without limit, to be more fitting because in my life. No matter what, God has proven to be faithful, His provision and grace more than sufficient. He lavishes His love on me and has throughout my life (1 John 3:1). All that has been required of me is to be open to growth and to be patient within the process of change. While I work toward a positive attitude in this, it doesn't always come easy. There are plenty of times when I'm disappointed at my lack of patience. The process can be so challenging and those nearest and dearest to me are the ones who suffer. If I don't feel well or am discouraged, they know it. Despite my behavior, they have been supportive and patient with me. This most recent cancer diagnosis and treatment has been a growing experience, to be sure. But growth always comes with some amount of pain, doesn't it?

"And God is able to provide you with every blessing in abundance, so that by always having enough of everything, you may share abundantly in every good work." 2 Corinthians 9:8. This passage is particularly beautiful to me. It reminds me that in the midst of the most trying times, of brokenness or pain, when I feel as if I have nothing to give, God's blessings to me are abundant and I will always have more than I need so I can share the goodness.

I choose not to live my life with the mindset of poverty or as a victim, but rather with a mindset of abundance and blessing. While I know my body's tendency toward anxiety and sensitivity to stress, my spirit and my mind are set on the goodness of God. Not just today, when I am starting to feel strong again, but every day. There is more to life than the moment, but I want to live each moment purposefully. I remain open to the lessons of growth and pain. I receive blessings from a good God. I share goodness with those around me. After all, "[S]he who has God lacks nothing. God alone [lavishes]."

7/9/15
I Wish It Were Always Summer
in Northern Michigan

July 4, 2015

We are wrapping up our family vacation here in beautiful Cheboygan, Michigan. This is where I grew up and where my parents still reside. Northern Michigan is paradise in summertime!

Five years ago, all three of my siblings and I, along with our families, were together at my parents' home for the summer holiday. We determined then that we would do our very best to make the 4th of July an annual event. Having all four Fenlon kids together in the same place at the same time was such a significant event (it had been *years*) that we all expressed the desire to make this a tradition.

Unfortunately, time, money, work schedules, and distance make this difficult. While my family and I have been able to manage to make it four years out of the last five, my other siblings have had a more difficult time making the trip back.

We truly enjoy spending time with my parents, Aunt Betty, Emillie, and the Kwiatkowski gang, and any other family or friends we are able to connect with while we are there. It's always a blast when "the cousins" are able to get together! There's nothing like quality time with family and there's nothing like summer in Northern Michigan.

The weather here is warm but mild. In Illinois where we live, it seems the temperature is either hot or cold, peak of summer or dead of winter. We are either running the air conditioning or the heater. Somehow the milder, transitional seasons of spring and fall have been cut out altogether. Not in Northern Michigan.

The colors still show themselves, bold and rich, on the leaves of the trees for weeks at a time beginning in late September and lasting sometimes into November. The air turns crisp and cool; "football weather," we call it. And in my hometown of Cheboygan, Michigan, there's nothing bigger than football.

The winters are long and cold. There is always lot of white, lovely snow. It doesn't turn brown or dingy the way snow in the city does. It remains clean and pristine. This could be due to the consistently fresh layer that falls almost daily. The lakes freeze over fairly early in the season, providing even more space for winter sports and adventure. Snowmobiling, ice fishing, and cross-country skiing are big in these parts.

After many months of this wonderland of ice and snow, the season gives way to spring. Ah, Spring, wet and wonderful! The snow slowly melts, leaving puddles in driveways and yards. Winter coats are exchanged for spring jackets. Umbrellas are pulled out of the closet and put to good use. The sun shows itself more and more throughout springtime. The ground begins to warm and brilliant green buds surface as a result. Boats begin to make their appearance on the lakes. It is a lovely time of year. But my favorite time of year in Northern Michigan is summertime. The plentiful waterways come alive with boats, jet skis, rafts, and swimmers. People you haven't seen all winter either return to the area or are now more readily venturing out of doors. The mornings and evenings are cool, inviting activity and exercise. The days are warm, thanks to an amazing sun that shows itself more frequently and whose rays and warmth are actually felt. There is usually a sweet lake effect breeze that sweeps through town. Where my parents live, five miles out of town, the air is often still, which makes the warmth of the sun even more substantial and effective. I love it.

The green grass of the yard; the tall grasses, wildflowers, and weeds of the meadow behind the house; the trees of the forest that surround their home; the isolation I despised as a teenager, now comfort me in adulthood. I love it.

This July 4th was one such idyllic summer day. As we sat on Main Street in front of River of Life Church where my parents pastor, I thought about how much I truly love this town and those who live here. The 4th of July parade participants marched along in front of me; my youngest child, William, sat on my lap. And as the bagpipes from Sault

Ste. Marie, Ontario, Canada came along, tears were streaming down my cheeks.

I visited my mom's naturopath last week. She did some talking with me and testing and found that my hormones were out of whack. "You get upset over the littlest things, don't you?" she asked. I confirmed this. She also found that only about 2% of my sleep is deep, reparative REM sleep. "You must be exhausted!" she empathized. Again, I was able to confirm this and told her of my irregular sleep patterns. All in all, the visit served to confirm some things I already knew, proved to me I'm not just overly emotional or crazy, highlighted some issues I wasn't aware of, and ways to address all of the above.

So as I sat at the 4th of July parade with tears in my eyes, I opened my heart to the bittersweet moment. "*If only I could save time, make a moment last longer than just 'a moment',*" I thought. And with that, the bagpipers had moved on and the racecar displayed on the tow truck came along with radio blaring. My idyllic moment had passed.

As the truck and racecar with loud music approached, William began to bounce on my lap in rhythm to the music. I wiped away my tears as I began to laugh with joy that the child in my lap showed his enjoyment and contentment in *this* moment.

I realize each moment holds something special for us; gifts wrapped in varied packages. I don't want to throw away a gift before unwrapping it just because I don't care for the packaging!

Summer in Northern Michigan is fantastic and in some ways I truly wish it could always be summertime there. But I wouldn't want to forfeit the beauty that comes with the fall, winter, or spring in order to maintain summer. I want all that creation has to give and to experience each moment of life, open to what it holds.

7/10/15
I Have to Tell it Like a Story

I have to tell this like a story; it's easier for me to relay the details in this way, without getting overly emotional...

"It's getting tougher," I told Pete through my tears and from the crook of his neck where I had hidden my face.

We stood in the middle of the exam room where the surgeon had just left us. Today was the day I had hoped to be scheduling my surgery and to have a clear plan to end this cancer treatment. But that was not to be. These two days in Skokie, which I had anticipated would be light and easy, were by no means either.

Thursday was IV Vitamin C at The Block Center. I was supposed to be receiving Herceptin (a Her2 blocker) by IV and was to receive it once every three weeks for the next year. However, because of a lowered ejection fraction and some symptoms involving my heart (as explained in "The Other Side of Struggle"), it was being withheld. The doctors want to see if my heart recovers after taking a break from the drug. I had a repeat echocardiogram on Monday and we will wait for the results of that test before resuming the treatment. In the meantime, I received a vitamin cocktail by IV. While at The Center I also met with Dr. Block and Dr. Kahn, my oncologist. Before my last chemo treatment, Dr. Kahn had reduced the dose of my chemo by 50% and said that if this reduction did not reduce or resolve my side effects, that it could be my last/final treatment. After experiencing all of the same side effects, along with the recurrence of another issue I had thought resolved, I assumed I was done with chemo in this case. Yesterday, when I met with Dr. Block and Dr. Kahn, they both implored me to have the sixth treatment as prescribed. They asked me to at least consider it. I agreed that I would. Through tears and with a cracking voice, I expressed my concerns about all the side effects as well as my uneasiness regarding the toxicity of adding yet another chemo treatment to an already weakened heart and body.

Dr. Block laid out fair and substantiated arguments for the sixth treatment, based on the information he had available to him. He addressed my concerns and stated that ultimately the decision was mine and he would continue to help me either way. He is intelligent and kind, and I am thankful to have him on my team.

I struggled to relax as we left The Center that night. Pete reminded me that a decision does not need to be made immediately. I should take the time to relax, pray, and seek peace, he encouraged. Every day, this man reminds me of his unconditional love and support. Pete is amazing and so patient with me. I'm so blessed by this man. I woke up this morning after a typically restless night. I successfully slept four hours at the outset of the night, woke up and had trouble getting back to sleep, finally to enjoy two full hours of sleep just before having to get up. I awoke with a smile, climbed out of bed, and thought out loud, "This is going to be a great day!" The weather matched my mood: sunny, bright, warm, and pleasantly breezy.

We made it to the doctor's office early for a visit to my plastic surgeon and were seen on time. It was perfect. Once the doctor examined me, the visit went downhill. Here's the long and short of it: the type of reconstruction surgery (DIEP or Tram Flap) I had wanted to have is no longer a viable option for me because of my weight loss due to chemo. This news was devastating. Since my first appointment with the surgeon three months ago, I had been talking myself into a surgery that I felt was the lesser of the evils. At this moment, I was being forced to rethink everything I had been considering and planning for.

At this point, I haven't come to any conclusions. These decisions are weighing heavily on me. I feel very responsible. Responsible to do what is best not only for myself, but also for my husband and children. I'm trying to rest and not rush, to seek peace in my decision-making. While I feel overwhelmed and wish I had a lighted path before me, I am clear on two things. One, there are no guarantees, whatever I choose. And two, regardless of any decision I might make, I am not the one ultimately in control here. We might like to think that we have control, but truly the only thing we have control over is our response to whatever and whoever comes to us in life.

As we drove home from Skokie, a song came into my head and I began to sing words that brought comfort in the midst of the emotional storm. "I lift my eyes up unto the mountains—where does my help come from? My help comes from You, Maker of heaven, Creator of the earth." Psalm 121:1-2. I accept this comfort and I continue to seek peace.

Sarah Fenlon Falk

7/26/15
Picture Everyone Bald

My hair is growing back. It's salt and pepper in color and growing just around the rim of my head. The top is still bald. Perhaps the hair there is blonde because it's very soft to the touch. I'm trusting God for a full head of hair one day soon!

I'm feeling stronger the more I am able to eat. Each day I have more energy to be active. Sometimes I overdo it and push myself beyond the limit, something I used to do before I was diagnosed (again) with cancer. I wonder if pushing myself "beyond" and experiencing that stress and overwhelming is part of what provided an environment for cancer to return to my body in the first place.

In my private practice, I preach to my clients about setting boundaries, maintaining appropriate limits within relationships and with themselves. These boundaries can mean learning to say no, or taking time for oneself, setting limits and putting a cap on time or emotion spent on someone else. Life without limits can lead to feeling overwhelmed, exhausted, and bitter.

161

As my hair grows back and I have more energy, I feel like I'm rediscovering myself. While I feel renewed in some sense, I see much of the old ways coming back into play. Pete has to remind me once again to "stop doing things and just rest." I've never been good at setting boundaries with myself in that way. So now that I am returning to strength, I am nervous; nervous that I won't remember the lessons learned and will just charge ahead with life at full speed.

I'm also unsettled about the way others will treat me. It is simply amazing the amount of compassion and empathy that is poured out on a person who is ill. As for me, the amount of support, love, and prayers that have been lavished upon me is so meaningful and healing. I appreciate it. I receive it with gratitude.

Even people I don't know are so very kind to me when they see my bald head. After all, it may be safe to assume that nine times out of ten, a person with a bald head is most likely undergoing chemotherapy and/or radiation treatment for cancer. Seeing a bald head is often a signal that someone is sick and really going through a difficult time. When I am a recipient of such directed kindness, it causes me to wonder what will happen when my hair grows back. What will happen when strangers can't see the difficult healing journey I am on because my head doesn't provide evidence of it? Will I be an annoyance or simply just another stranger? Because that's what strangers are to me sometimes. I hate to admit it, but it's true. I get annoyed with people. I fail to remember that everyone has a story. We are all on a journey of healing,

healing from one thing or another. The least we can do is remember that and to give grace and have patience with one another.

I was discussing these things and confessing my shortcoming to my mom the other day. She suggested, somewhat jokingly, "Maybe we should picture everyone bald." While we chuckled about it, we also realized there was something to that. The empathy/sympathy I tend to receive because of the obvious illustration of my journey should be the same empathy/sympathy extended to all, regardless of their appearance. I would love to be that person full of grace and compassion. I can be that person at times, but when I am in a hurry and the line is long, I lose all sense of empathy.

This is abundantly clear to me: I do not want to return to the harried, hurried, and harsh person that I can become when I am lacking boundaries, failing to protect myself from overworking and overachieving. Learning to set clear boundaries with myself may be one of the major lessons I will learn during this time. To preserve the level of self-care that I have implemented since my most recent cancer diagnosis is paramount. That will involve reserving time for my family and myself; to limit the expectations I put upon myself to "do." I can see clearly that when I am moving at a measured pace, fully present in the moment, I am a better wife, mother, friend, and a more empathetic stranger.

So as I continue the process of learning to set healthy boundaries for my own wellbeing, I will also picture everyone bald. Because we all have a story, and I truly desire to treat others the way I have been treated throughout this cancer story.

8/2/15
The "Power" in Empowerment

As I look ahead to surgery in the coming month or two, there are two surgeons on my team: Dr. Knaus, the oncology surgeon who will perform the lumpectomy or mastectomy (depending on what we decide); and Dr. Pavone, the plastic surgeon who will perform the initial reconstructive surgery. Both men were referrals from The Block Center and both have proven to be wonderful.

Let me just say that when you're sitting in the exam room with a pink paper shirt on (a mini-gown that opens in front and doesn't even cover your belly button) the last thing you want is for your doctor to come into the room and make you feel even more awkward. And that is why I am so thankful for Dr. John Knaus. The first time Pete and I met him, about four months ago, he was so very kind and thoughtful. Pete and I sat and talked with him about my situation, of course, but then talked about our joys, families, activities, and so on. He shared about himself as well, his family and personal love of fishing. At the end of our visit (it didn't feel like a "doctor appointment"), he sent me off with his personal cell phone number and a kiss on the cheek.

Wednesday was no different. Greeted with a firm handshake and a kiss on the cheek, I felt my heart swell from the moment we said hello. I had been nervous about this appointment, but with that greeting, all anxiety melted away. We caught up on life over the last four months, including the course of my chemotherapy treatments, his weight loss that I had remarked on, and how my children were doing, as well as to discuss specifics for my upcoming surgery.

As per my recollection, I had been directed, by every oncology surgeon I'd previously spoken with, toward a bilateral mastectomy. The reconstruction part was always up to me; however, the mastectomy part seemed like a given as far as any health care practitioner I'd talked to was concerned. Believing that I had no options in this matter left me feeling depressed and forced into something with which I wasn't completely comfortable.

"What have you decided?" he asked me.

I confess I couldn't speak for a moment; I was so taken aback by the question. As he waited for me to reply, I explained to him that I had been under the impression that I didn't have a choice or decision to make; that I *had* to have a mastectomy. He kindly and calmly explained that I did have options and he laid them out for me:

1. Lumpectomy with close monitoring due to the risk of recurrence; 2. Unilateral mastectomy with or without

reconstruction with close monitoring; or, 3. Bilateral mastectomy with or without reconstruction and moderate monitoring, because this procedure would provide a 98% chance of a"cure." (Cure is in quotations because there is no defined cure for cancer. A person who has survived a cancer diagnosis by five years post-treatment is considered "cured;" however, all treatment for cancer is experimental. I feel it's very important to clarify this.)

Dr. Knaus assured me whatever I decide to do he will work with me. If I choose to act conservatively with choice 1 or 2, he explained I would be watched carefully. He further explained that if I wish to distance myself from the medical community and to carry on with life, then the most aggressive approach, a bilateral mastectomy, would be best.

For the remainder of the appointment he took time to answer my questions as I sought more specific details regarding incisions and scarring, length of surgery and recovery, and anything else I could think to ask him. He provided the facts and was honest in giving his opinion when it was solicited. It was an open and honest conversation. He made eye contact with me, called me by name, and waited patiently for me to answer his questions.

Leaving the exam room, I noticed how light I felt. I definitely felt better when leaving his office than I had coming in. I made it a point to tell the office staff how much I appreciated their kindness, as well as that of the doctor. It makes all the difference in the world to have kind people to work with when in the midst of a health crisis.

I went into my doctor's appointment on Wednesday railing against the idea of having to have at least a unilateral mastectomy and knowing most would advise bilateral, given my genetic risk factors. I left the doctor's office almost certain that I would be choosing a bilateral mastectomy, given my genetic risk factors, and feeling confident and good about the decision. Dr. Knaus had given me my power back. He handed me the reins and told me to decide. He gave me clear options and answered all my questions so that I would have all of the information I would need in order to make a decision. In doing so, I was led right back to the recommended course of action.

Given all that I have learned about cancer, wellness, and my body over the last several months, I remain torn with this decision on some level. Torn because I know there are no guarantees that I won't get cancer again, whether I act aggressively or not. Torn because I know that genetics are not a road map to the future, and there is so much happening in the medical world regarding treatment and prevention that it is incredible.

At the end of the day, however, I will make a decision based on the treatment of the day and the information provided me; I will make a decision for my husband and my children, the choice that is likely to afford me the most time possible with them.

As I look ahead toward surgery in the next couple of months, I'm so thankful for my team. I am thankful for the doctors, nurse, therapists, family, and friends. I am so very grateful to God for the way I have been led and cared for on this healing journey.

8/9/15
No Simple Decisions

I saw my second surgeon on Friday, second surgeon because someone as special as I am must have not one, but two surgeons. *I'm kidding.* Two surgeons because one is the oncology surgeon who performs the mastectomy and the other is the plastic surgeon who begins the reconstruction. My visit with my oncology surgeon last week had rekindled a lot of confidence in me as chronicled in "Picture Everyone Bald." I was hoping to keep that momentum going, but it didn't happen that way at this visit. While I was at the office for almost an hour, a good portion of that time was spent on pre-operative necessities such as filling out paperwork, photos, and question and answer time with the office nurse. I spent about a quarter of that time with the doctor to discuss what conclusions I'd come to and any concerns that still lingered.

I've come to learn that a mastectomy isn't simply "a mastectomy," but there are many different ways to approach the procedure. I've also learned that reconstruction isn't simply "reconstruction," but there are many decisions to be made regarding the type of reconstruction with a number of possible outcomes. If a patient chooses reconstruction, that process is usually (not always) begun at the time of the mastectomy. That is why I have met with two surgeons in the span of one week and two days.

For a woman faced with the need for a mastectomy, there are a number of decisions to be made: First, will it be a single mastectomy or bilateral? The answer to this will typically depend upon the risk involved in keeping the other breast intact. If there are genetic factors that heighten the risks, as is my case, then a bilateral mastectomy is typically recommended or chosen.

Secondly, will it be a nipple-sparing and/or skin-sparing (just what they sound like) mastectomy? This typically depends upon the patient's pre-operative size and shape. Sometimes the type of cancer/tumor is a factor in this decision for doctor and patient.

Third question is: with or without reconstruction? This, as I've already explained, is a complex question. It's been a very difficult decision for me to make, and even though I've made a decision, I feel like I haven't *really* made a decision. For me, at my age and activity level, reconstruction is a given. There are many women who have chosen the mastectomy without reconstruction who utilize prosthetic bras and are content with their decision. That was something I could not imagine for myself. So, reconstruction it is.

At my last visit with my plastic surgeon, I was dealt a

devastating blow. I touched on this in "I Have to Tell it Like a Story". When I was told, way back in March, that a mastectomy was my best option to deal with my cancer and given the risk factors involved, I spent much time talking myself into the idea. I read and re-read about the different types of surgeries, including reconstruction. I asked questions, and then read some more. I looked at pictures and read and prayed for peace. I finally settled on bilateral mastectomy with DIEP flap reconstruction. To put it very plainly, the reconstruction would be to take excess fat and tissue from my abdomen and relocate it to build the breast mound on my chest. This was a comfortable decision for me because I liked the idea of the reconstructed breast being from another part of my own body (no implant, prosthetics, etc.). It seemed the more natural choice. The surgery, as it was explained to me, is not an easy one, as not only fat tissue but also veins would need to be transplanted. All in all, the surgery would take about eight to ten hours. I spent much time preparing myself for this and mentally/emotionally reached a place where I was peaceful with the choice. At the end of June, at my last appointment with the plastic surgeon, all of that changed. Due to being unable to eat during chemotherapy, I had lost all of that fat that was going to be transplanted and was no longer an eligible candidate for the DIEP flap reconstruction. I couldn't discuss any other options at that time. I was in tears and could not make myself stop crying.

It's been a month now. It really only took about a week's

time for me to collect myself once again and consider my options, now limited, for reconstruction. It came down to implants. There are two types of implants, silicone or saline. Not only that but the size, timing, and placement of the implants are other factors to consider. Some women are candidates for direct implant, meaning, at the time of the mastectomy, implants are placed and there are no further surgeries required. Other women have to take into consideration the effects of future radiation treatments on their skin, such as a tightening or toughening of the skin, which can impact the size or type of implant they would receive. In such cases, reconstruction is often postponed but tissue expanders may be placed to stretch the skin as far as it can be stretched at time of surgery with the plan to expand more, once radiation treatment has been completed.

Since I will not be having radiation, I was hoping for a direct implant at the time of the mastectomy. I am not a fan of surgery and have had many in my day. If I could avoid one more, that's what I would do. However, at my appointment Friday when I brought up my wish for a direct implant, I was told that would not be the best option for me. Expanders that would be placed at the time of mastectomy, then filled slowly over the course of the next few weeks after surgery, were the recommended course of action. After the expanders were filled, another surgery to place the implants would be performed. The second surgery in the reconstruction process is just another step toward detail work: two or more outpatient surgeries to complete the look. All in all, this reconstruction process spans the course of about one year. My thought/feeling of, "I just want to have the surgery and be done with it" does not work in this scenario.

I've heard other women talk about their surgical decisions and they seem so confident in their decisions. I don't feel confident at all as I've tried different decisions on for size. I haven't found a decision that feels right just yet. I know what I should do, or even must do, but something is nagging.

Despite the nagging, I am so thankful for kind and patient surgeons who take the time to answer my questions, allow me to get to know them a bit so that I feel more comfortable, and who are skilled at what they do. I know I'm in good hands and in a good place in this process, but I've come to realize a difficult truth: there are just no simple decisions here. So I will do what I've done all along and continue to seek the peace. I'm near it, I know, but complicated decisions just take time.

8/12/15
Bridle This Blessing

I'm preparing for a colonoscopy tomorrow. There are worse things. But I cannot say how many times I have had to remind myself that I cannot eat today. (liquid diet until midnight, then NPO). It's amazing how often throughout the day I have gone to put something in my mouth reflexively. As I was making breakfast and lunch for my boys, while I was cleaning the kitchen, and now as I sit at the kitchen table to write and there is a bowl of fresh-out-of-the- garden peas nearby, the urge to eat has been a tough one to overcome.

The good news is that after four months of struggling to get food into my mouth past chemo- riddled taste buds, I am now able to eat. Slowly over the past few weeks, my taste buds have been healing. Food went from being abhorrent, to just not awful, to most things are all right, and now everything tastes good and I am Out. Of. Control.

The last few days, I have found myself eating anything and everything that crosses my path. It's a luxury and a pleasure that I have been missing, and I am not holding back now. This is not good for a number of reasons. First, sugar feeds cancer. Since I am in the business currently of working to rid my body of cancer, this sugar consumption is counterproductive to my health and wellbeing. Second, I am diabetic and know well enough to limit my sugar and simple carbohydrate intake. Finally, I am rapidly gaining back some of the inches I had lost during chemotherapy. While I could afford to gain back some, it is the bloat from eating foods that are toxic that is the issue. I cannot afford to neglect the health of my body in such a way.

As I contemplate the blessing of being able to taste food for real and to eat without choking, I realize I must work to bridle this blessing. Bridle: to control or hold back; restrain; curb. If I do not exercise self-control, discipline, and restraint here, it will be detrimental. In order to do so, I must plan. Before my diagnosis, I had worked very hard to become structured in my eating and meal planning. I didn't hit the mark 100% of the time but I did a very decent job of it. Now it feels like a free-for-all and I *want to* allow it. It's time for a visit to my nutritionist.

I am thankful for taste buds that have been restored. I am blessed with returning strength. I am also very grateful for the lessons I have learned this go-around with a cancer diagnosis. I have learned so much about nutrition, my body and how to care for it, healing, and wellness. Because of this knowledge, I will make wise and healthy choices. I will bridle this blessing.

8/17/15
The Number of My Days

I've been feeling so exhausted lately. I'm almost certain it is from sheer mental and emotional overload. The recent days have been filled with doctor's appointments, trying to arrange and rearrange schedules for more appointments, and an upcoming surgery, all the while planning to send my oldest baby off to kindergarten. The last two events are ones I am not in the least prepared for. How could I be?

I read something about how surprised by time we (and "we" being everyone) tend to be. We remark about how fast summer has gone, how quickly babies and children grow, and how holidays seem to run together these days. But what is more natural than the passing of time? Yet I am one of the first to make any one of the mentioned remarks and to truly be amazed by it. When I consider these things, I become almost frantic and sad. I can never have yesterday back. Bobby will never be a "preschooler" again. The phases my children have passed through are gone forever now. That makes me sad.

Forgive me for being graphic, but when I consider the permanence of cutting off a body part or two as a step in my cancer treatment/prevention, it makes me sad. I have actually envisioned waking up from surgery crying, realizing that what was done can never be undone.

So perhaps part of this exhaustion I'm feeling is a byproduct of the grieving process. Grief is a natural and arduous journey through various emotions all in relation to the loss of something or someone. (My definition.) Our society tends to take what is known as ambiguous loss for granted; those losses that are not directly apparent. For instance, it's obvious one would grieve the death of a loved one or pet, but not always "obvious" to grieve an unfulfilled dream or the sale of a childhood home. In my case, I'm grieving a number of things: the loss of health for starters, but also the disruption of my family life, and what will be lost after a bilateral mastectomy, to name a few.

To balance out the sadness (not dismiss it or minimize it), I have made it a point to look at the flip side of the coin. This deep sadness has led me to deeper relationships; grief has taught me greater empathy; frustration has led me to seek peace in solitude; and disruption has stirred up creativity. I bless God for the fact that my family is healthy. I am so thankful for an abounding support system. There is beauty in the midst of pain and emotional exhaustion.

When I become anxious about the fleeting passage of time, I realize that it is wise for me to learn to be more mindful and present of and in each moment. As I have been reflecting on these lessons, I find these words coming to mind "teach me to number my days." To me, this is a measured approach to mortality, a reminder that every moment is rich. Instead of whipping myself into a frenzy so as not to "waste a day," I am savoring each moment. I am not rushing in to tomorrow. I am not bemoaning the passage of another day. I simply am. I know that I will not *be* forever. But right now, I am.

"Lord, remind me how brief my time on earth will be. Remind me that my days are numbered – how fleeting my life is. You have made my life no longer than the width of my hand. My entire lifetime is just a moment to you; at best, each of us is but a breath. We are merely moving shadows, and all our busy rushing ends in nothing. We heap up wealth, not knowing who will spend it. And so, Lord, where do I put my hope? My only hope is in You."Psalm 39:4-7 NLT.

So, after another day of mental and emotional exhaustion, I've decided to rest here, understanding and being content with the fact that my life is but a breath. I don't need to rush around, gaining nothing and missing precious moments. I put my hope in God and find peace in the moment.

8/23/15
Life and Death, Daily

I've been kicking around thoughts about life and death these days. I say this knowing I run the risk of sounding irreverent or even flippant when the idea of death is introduced. That's how it is in our society. Death is a taboo topic. I will admit I've been afraid to say the word a time or two, or to allow myself to think too deeply on the matter, because I didn't want to "jinx" myself. After all, our thoughts affect our lives in very real and lasting ways. But recently Pete brought a book home to me from the library, *Being Mortal* by Atul Gawande. This book, as you might expect given the title, takes a look at how different cultures approach mortality and what impact our views about death have on our lives. I only made it about three chapters in before it was due back. (I was chewing on it, not just breezing through, *and* I have four children and two jobs!) What I read floored me. I had even read the introduction, something I will admit I usually skip. Atul Gawande is a doctor. As someone who has both worked in the medical field and been a patient of it, I have seen and experienced its shortcomings. Dr. Gawande has too, and focuses on some of the dehumanizing practices in the industry. He also shares his thoughts and experiences regarding the beauty that can be found in caring and being cared for, living and dying. I think I need to own this book.

Dr. Gawande's words triggered more thoughts about dying for me. Not the fear that I am going to die, or the idea that I need to prepare myself for a near and untimely death, but, to try to acknowledge death more openly. To approach aging, living, dying with a confidence, a strength, and dignity. Death is a very natural part of life. Perhaps it's easy for me to say that as, after completing chemotherapy treatment, I have received an "all clear" from a PET scan and breast MRI exam. Yes, good news! And I thank God! Yet, even now as I am planning surgery as part of my treatment and prevention, I'm reminded there are no guarantees in this life. I am given the moment and hope to cherish it, not let it pass me by.

So I allowed myself to contemplate the reality of death being a natural part of life. One of the interesting things to consider about living and dying is that we carry around death and life in our physical bodies every day. Our bodies experience different types of cellular death moment by moment. In the event of an injury, the cellular death is of a traumatic nature called necrosis, a result of acute cellular injury. Apoptosis is a highly regulated form of cellular death, a controlled process that is for the benefit of our life cycle. Our bodies experience the birth of new cells as well. The rates vary. (If our cells fail to die regularly as in apoptosis, but instead continue to produce, a tumor is formed.) Life and death on a cellular level.

I also considered this daily experience of life and death on a spiritual level. I recalled a verse I had been given by way of encouragement while I was going through my chemotherapy treatments and one I've used during past difficult times: "We are hard pressed on every side, but not crushed; perplexed, but not in despair; persecuted, but not abandoned; struck down, but not destroyed." 2 Corinthians 4:8-9. But it was the next verse that really caught my attention this time. Verse 10, "We always carry around in our body the death of Jesus, so that the life of Jesus may also be revealed in our body."

For the Apostle Paul writing this passage, it was because of the death and resurrection of Christ that he was intent on dying to himself, putting aside his personal desires and expectations so that the life and message of Christ was what was seen in him. Dying to self and surrendering whatever would be to the strength and will of the God he served.

I believe this is the message for me in the midst of all these thoughts of living and dying: choose to live life well, to the fullest, while dying to my own expectations of how long life should be and everything I would want life to be. This allows me to move graciously forward into an uncharted future, holding all that I have and am with open hands, and making precious each and every moment. Of course I have wishes and a will of my own. I have expectations and desires for this life. But as I integrate those times and places of frustration and pain, I will grow. I will find beauty in the pain and pleasure, the living and dying.

9/4/15
Saying Goodbye to the Girls

I began writing this in April and finished in September, a long good-bye, if you will. It's difficult to express, even now, five weeks after my surgery, what it is and has been like to decide to remove a part of my body. I must admit I have had second thoughts, doubts. In those moments, I have to remind myself of the labor-intensive, prayer-filled, thought-provoking, arduous decision-making process that I journeyed through to get to the place where I felt I had the best information and the best team to carry out what I needed for my health, wellness, and longevity. I can't take it back. What's done is done and regret has no place in healing, the healing process, or in the peace of a moment.

These have been my thoughts over the course of five months on saying goodbye to my breasts: We have a history. I remember when they started growing. They fed all four of my children. They have been a part of my pain and pleasure for forty-one years. It's a strange sort of grieving, contemplating our parting. Saying goodbye to something that

184

has been with me all of my life; a part of me. When I had bone cancer in 1991, I had to contemplate the possibility of losing my left leg. Before I went into surgery, the doctors were not sure if they would be able to save my leg. So the day after I turned 18, I went into surgery not knowing if I would come out with both legs. But contemplating the loss of a leg versus the loss of two breasts is a very different thing. I wonder how this loss could affect my sexuality. It's such a personal/private experience, unlike a leg. I cringe to think about how many times I have said, "If I ever had breast cancer I would just chop them off." Until you've sat in that office and had the doctor measure you and show you on your own chest where they will cut and remove, you cannot know that you would do it. I regret every time I ever made that statement.

Having breast cancer is such a personal and private thing. People get cancer all the time but when it's in a private area, it makes the conversation a little more sensitive. Many people are private about their medical status anyway. That's something that never really concerned me. Much of what I've gone through has been physically obvious to the causal onlooker anyway. I've never thought it necessary to try to hide or conceal what I'm going through. But it is strange to talk about my breasts in such a way with so many. I decided early on in this journey that I would be straightforward and honest in the conversation about my experience for the support and encouragement of others, and I feel it's important that I continue to be candid and genuine, even in the midst of these intimate aspects.

As I prepare to say goodbye to "the girls," I am sad and reflective, remembering all this body has brought me through and considering with hope all the things an (altered) body will experience in the future.

9/6/15
Firsts and Lasts

It's been a couple weeks of firsts and lasts around our household. I've been very emotional. The first of the firsts was our oldest boy Bobby losing a tooth. It wasn't as dramatic a thing as I remember tooth removal being when I was little and losing them. He was eating breakfast one day and his loose tooth just fell out. This being a Sunday morning, Bobby requested to take the thing to church. So, mother that I am, I found a tiny ziplock baggie-type thing (the size used to hold a spare button for a shirt), punched a hole, tied a string, and he proudly wore that tooth around his neck all morning. He was sure to put it under his pillow that night in hopes of the tooth fairy bringing him "a coin" in exchange for his tooth. I thank Jake and the Neverland Pirates for setting the expectations low by suggesting that the tooth fairy brings "a coin" for a tooth. Bobby did, however, receive a dollar bill *and* a coin (a quarter) from the tooth fairy for his first tooth. A second tooth followed that first tooth not more than two weeks later.

This brings us to another first: kindergarten. I find it difficult to fathom the passing of time, which has brought us from returning home from the hospital with a tiny, helpless baby to then dropping said baby off at a building miles from home for multiple hours in a day with people we have barely met. And all of this is apparently "normal." I can't express how nervous and sad I was leading up to that day. My son, on the other hand, has been looking forward to his first day of school for months, possibly longer. We drove him to school and I was able to walk him to his classroom. He was cool as a cucumber. Once inside, he behaved as if he knew exactly what he was doing and was eager to do it. I shed a few tears as I left him there that day. Those tears were for me, not for him. He has enjoyed each day of school more than the last. I'm so thankful he likes it.

The same week we took our oldest son to kindergarten was the week that our youngest son, William, turned two. Just a day or two before his birthday, I entered my bedroom and took inventory of a pile of carriers and books stacked there (waiting to go to another family by way of eBay or The Baby- Wearing Swap on Facebook) and saw in that pile the baby book I had bought for William before he was born—the wrapper removed, no entries made. I have a million or more pictures of the boy but have yet to write in his baby book. (All milestones are documented on the kitchen calendar from last year and this). So we officially said good-bye to the baby stage. This guy is a little boy, but for the diapers and bedtime miney (pronounced mine-ee, what the twins called their pacifiers and the name stuck). Our last baby is growing up so fast. He does his darnedest to keep up with his three older brothers. He does a pretty good job of it too. Counting, reciting ABC's, learning bedtime prayers, singing songs, playing games, and navigating tech (iPhones, iPads, etc.) like he was born with them in his hands. It wasn't long ago I was tucking him into his little carrier at the park, feeding him from my own body, watching him learn to roll over, sit up, pull up, stand. Again, the passage of time confuses me. Looking back at pictures of this child as a baby leaves me in awe and wonder: *was that a hundred years ago, or just yesterday?*

And as I contemplate these firsts and lasts, I consider the firsts and lasts I am experiencing with this body of mine. Though my PET scan and breast MRI showed that I am clear of cancer at this time, my genetic risk factors are so high that a bilateral mastectomy will be done a week from Monday. Preparing for the surgery has been an interesting process thus far. Really, I feel like I've been preparing for it since I found out I had cancer back in February. I've been gathering my facts, talking to people, reading, etc. But I've also been going through a phase that looks a lot like the nesting phase in pregnancy. I'm making sure everything is just so because once the surgery is done, it will be weeks, almost months, before I'll be back to full capabilities. I'm trying to grasp what will be happening to my body in the course of this surgery next week. It's quite an emotional thing. At the very least, because I've taken for granted the idea that when my soul leaves this body, this body will still have all its original parts. In 1991, when going in for surgery to remove the tumor in my left femur, not knowing whether I would come out of the procedure with a leg, I never considered actually losing the leg. I assumed, or perhaps I was unable to think otherwise, that I would come out with my leg intact. And I did. But now, with breast cancer and in this upcoming surgery, the doctors will remove them, parts will not be spared. In my mind, I have made peace with the fact that this is for the best. I sense it's the right move to make. However, I'm also acutely aware that I am spending the last days with all my original body parts. I am blessed beyond belief that there are surgeons (artists, really) who can remove what is diseased or holds potential threat and replace it with form and shape that, once healed, will restore a sense of balance and normality to this body. After September 14, I will never be the same again. I'm not the same person I was yesterday, for that matter. Last days are being celebrated and mourned here, but there is also expectancy, a hope, of firsts yet to come.

9/11/15
Is It Just Me?

In preparation for surgery, I have weighed myself down with a long list of unreasonable tasks that will be impossible for me to complete in the next two days. It's much like the nesting phase during pregnancy when an expectant mother feels the need to have every single detail of house and home "just so" before the little babe arrives. Of course, just like the expectant mother, I have absolutely no energy or time, not because I am great with child but because I have been sick with a cold for a week. Feeling under the weather and exhausted from overdoing it always makes me emotional. I've experienced a wide range of emotions during the past week or two. There have been moments when I feel like I'm absolutely losing my mind, which causes me to ask, "Is it just me?"

Is it just me, or does every woman who has made the colossal decision to amputate her breasts in the name of survival experience an identity crisis? Not that my breasts contain my identity, but they have been a part of my human experience for forty- one years, and the thought of losing them is a difficult one. They are a part of what makes my whole, and "parts" are often taken for granted.

It won't matter when I'm dead, someday— years from now, God willing. But, I've always just assumed that I would leave this earth bearing all of the parts with which I entered in. Is it just me, or do others think about that too?

Obviously, the body I am living in today is not identical to the one conceived over forty-two years ago. Things have changed and grown in this body since its arrival on November 7, 1973 when a 6- pound, 13-ounce baby girl was born. This body has been through a lot in the last forty-one (almost forty- two) years: physical pain as well as physical pleasure, a body being pushed to its limits for sports or personal goal, pregnancies, and the birthing of tiny humans, and surgeries, all in the name of living and life. How can I approach this unnatural step in my evolution, an event that, given any other circumstance, I would decline? It feels as though I am facing a situation that will leave me unfamiliar with myself. I'm feeling overwhelmed by emotions and thoughts, so I task myself into distraction.

My task list also comes out of a place of not knowing, specifically not knowing what my post- surgical physical capabilities will be. I'm getting all the heavy lifting done before my surgery just in case it takes months to get back to it afterward. I feel the need to get *everything* in order and in place because of the nagging "just in case" feeling. I'm not certain what all or what exactly I am concerned will happen, but that unknown is driving me. Heading toward a major, life-altering surgery, I'm keeping busy and there is no limit on expectations of myself. Is it just me?

9/13/15
Hurdles and Bumps

"Just another hurdle on the road to recovery."
I ran track in high school for one year. It took me two years
to get the guts to go out for track, then after running one year,
I was diagnosed with bone cancer in my left femur and have
been unable to run since. I remember back in those days
during practice after a long day at school, we would run until
we couldn't run any more. Sitting there huffing and puffing,
trying to catch my breath, I would look at the hurdles set up
along the outside of the track for the hurdlers to practice. The
hurdles were so tall, about up to my chest, and I would think,
how in the heck can anyone jump over those? Most of the
female hurdlers were no bigger than I was, so I simply could
not fathom how they were able to get their legs apart wide
enough and foot up high enough to get over the thing. I loved
watching them practice, though; it was amazing to watch legs
propel faster than what seemed should be humanly possible,
legs stretched almost in a straight line—one ahead, one
behind—and up into the air with the hurdler. It almost looked

as though they were flying. And they might as well have been, as far as I was concerned

Here I am at the edge of my hurdle, the next bit to get through, the next hill to climb, the next thing to overcome. I'm not excited about having surgery. I will say I am excited about the time I will have off afterward, but not thrilled about having drainage tubes on either side of my body for a couple weeks, or the pain of incisions and manipulated muscles and temporary implants. I am looking forward to eliminating a potential threat to my health. And while I'll miss my kids while I'm in the hospital, and then miss playing and wrestling with them for a while after I return home, it will be worth it for the many more days I am hoping I will be able to be in their lives. That's the whole point of this hurdle: to buy more time. While I can't fathom what the next few days are going to bring, I am planning on pushing myself, like the hurdlers in practice at Cheboygan Area High School once did, and fly!

"Just another bump in the road of life." Yes, it is time for yet another one of these. Technically, two bumps, as a coworker's sister so astutely pointed out. (She's just had a double mastectomy so she's earned the right to joke like that!) I laughed when she said it. Two bumps because both breasts will be surgically removed (mastectomy) and reconstructed; "two bumps" because this isn't the last of the surgeries. In another several months (maybe about six) I will be having another surgery to put in the permanent implants. In the meantime, the expanders that will be placed under the chest muscle immediately after the mastectomy on Monday will be filled little by little to stretch the muscle. Then, once they have been stretched to an appropriate size the surgery for the permanent implants will be scheduled. Beyond that, in another several weeks, after surgical wounds are healed, the detail work of reconstruction will take place to create nipples and areolas.

All throughout the reconstruction process, I will be receiving Herceptin treatments by IV once every three weeks. Herceptin is the targeted therapy that is used to block the Her2 protein that was feeding the tumor in the first place. The issue with Herceptin is that it affects the heart. And since my heart has already been affected by previous chemotherapy from 1991-92, I have to be followed closely by an oncology cardiologist. Herceptin has also affected my heart and I have been forced to stop the treatment for a time to see if my heart would recover. It did, but I have sought the wisdom of an oncology cardiologist before continuing for the next year. As has been the case in my care, I was sent (by God and a Google search) to a wonderful doctor at the University of Chicago, Dr. DeCara. She was very kind, patient, and knowledgeable and seemed interested in my case as well. I'm very thankful to have added her to my team. After each Herceptin treatment, I will have an echocardiogram done and she will look it over to be sure the treatment does not do any further or lasting damage to my heart. The positive thing about the effect that Herceptin has on the heart is that the heart typically bounces back after discontinuing the treatment.

My visit with the cardiologist was a positive one, as was my visit to my GP this week. I didn't actually see the GP but instead saw his Nurse Practitioner, Liz, who has been on my team for a long time. I was being seen there for surgical clearance. And while I have had a cold for about a week now, everything else checked out and I was indeed cleared. Liz called yesterday to see if the cold was gone yet. As it is not, she ordered some medication for me to start immediately. Although I am tired, I must say that the symptoms have reduced since yesterday morning and I am feeling better. I'm nervous that I'll get to the hospital and because of my cold they will send me home again. If that's the case, then surgery will most likely be rescheduled for November. But, I'd rather wait than take any risks just because I want to be done with it. The anticipation is no easy thing to cope with, but I can wait if I must, if that's the safer option.

Now, as the day is so close, I find myself withdrawing a bit, getting frustrated very easily, and feeling as though there is not enough time in a day to get my tasks done and spend time with my children. Even though I won't be in the hospital for very long, I am feeling and acting as though I'll be away for weeks. Perhaps this is because I know my activities will be limited after the surgery, so I've been getting in all the chores, boy-wrestling, baby-lifting, and home-rearranging that I could handle in the last few days. Or perhaps it's because I know life will never be the same again. I will never be the same.

And now it's time to go to sleep and wake up to "the day before." Those days always go quickly. Instead of dwelling on the event to come, I think I'll visualize the hurdler, defying gravity, gracefully leaping over something that is almost as tall as they are and totally blowing the minds of onlookers. Yep. That's what I'll do.

Sarah Fenlon Falk

9/18/15
Heavy and Hollow

I had surgery on Monday, bilateral mastectomy and
beginning reconstruction. The pain upon waking was not at
all what I thought it would be. I felt sore, achy, and a little
pained, but nothing like the day after a C-section when I
would feel as if I was being torn apart from the inside out.
There was no nausea or vomiting either, also a new
experience for me. I usually get very sick with anesthesia and
was sure to stress this point with the team that spoke with me
prior to surgery. When discussing this issue with other nurse
friends of mine they suggested trying a scopolamine patch
during surgery. To put it plainly, scopolamine reduces
secretions. It is typically used for motion sickness, but also
with hospice patients who have fluid in their lungs, to assist
in maintaining comfortable, easy breathing. Aside from the
scopolamine patch, I'm not sure what other tricks the
anesthetists used, but whatever they did worked! It was a
monumental achievement as far as I was concerned.

The surgery was scheduled to last four to six hours, and

everyone was preparing my husband, Pete, to settle in for a long one, but in the end both procedures took a jot less than four hours together and both doctors were very pleased with the results. Preliminary findings suggested that the cancer had been eradicated by the chemotherapy prior to this surgery, this of course being the goal. All tissue and lymph nodes were sent to pathology for testing. My oncology surgeon said that he would be contacting us as soon as he had any word from pathology. I spent one night in the hospital and by the afternoon on Tuesday was headed home. It all happened so quickly.

When I arrived home I must say I was a bit scared of my children. I was so happy to see them but afraid of their energy and sudden movements. I couldn't use my arms to catch them or stop them from jumping at me. They are little boys and they do a lot of jumping and such: innocent, excited behavior of healthy little boys. But, I felt very standoffish with them and hated it. I wanted to pick my baby up and cuddle him close. He had a cold and was a bit whiney that afternoon when I came home. He wanted his mom and I wasn't able to hold him. My mom sat him on the couch next to me and I patted his little leg. That was about all I could do.

As much as it saddened me to have to be so protective of myself, as I've said, I was perhaps more nervous or apprehensive about getting hurt. So, my parents helped to buffer and Cindy came to take the boys to the park and for a couple of days this worked fairly well.

Pete, Mom, Dad, and Cindy would all ask how I was

doing these few days after coming home. I didn't know. My chest felt heavy and hollow. My emotions were void. I remarked to Pete and my mom how I thought it was strange that I wasn't feeling anything.

"Why are you surprised when you've had so many people praying that you would have peace?" Pete asked me. I couldn't argue. But then again, I wasn't sure I was feeling "peace." The truth was, I wasn't feeling much of anything at all. My emotions too were heavy and hollow. I could feel slight relief that the surgery was behind me and that I was home again. I was able to feel a bit of joy at seeing my children again, mixed in with that apprehension in trying not to overdo. But mostly my heart was heavy, emotions hollow, just like my chest.

By Thursday, my parents were packed and ready to go back to northern Michigan for the family wedding on Saturday. It was decided my youngest three boys would go with them. Bobby would stay behind so as not to miss school. Here was the part that I had been disappointed about from the start: missing out on the wedding and a mini-family reunion. Family I haven't seen in years would be there. In the course of time they would be in Michigan for the wedding, I would have three doctor appointments, making it virtually impossible for me to consider going with them. (Let alone the six-hour ride in the van just to get there!) No, it was not meant for me to go. I felt my eyes fill with tears and my heart hang even more heavily when they drove away that morning.

Even so, there was nothing for me to do but rest. So I

read, and wrote, and watched movies. My son went to school and my husband went to work. Cindy checked in on me. And I still didn't feel much of anything. I realized that I had not yet looked at the surgical site. Other than the heaviness and pain I feel in my chest, and caring for three drains that come from the sides of my body, in one sense I am unaware of what has happened to me. I haven't looked. I'm scared to look. So for today, I am heavy and hollow. Who knows what I'll be when I actually take a look.

9/26/15
Miracles in the Mess

There is much about life that seems messy right now. I'm not able to keep up with things around the house the way I typically would. Due to my lift restrictions, I can't do laundry as efficiently as I'd like. I'm a do-it-yourselfer and it's hard for me to ask friends and family to pick up the slack where I cannot keep up. Even my body looks and feels like a bit of a shambles right now. I had one drainage tube removed at my appointment on Friday. Praise be to God! I only have two drainage tubes to contend with now, one on the right side and one on the left. While they are irritating and cumbersome, I know that they are preventing infection and keeping my wounds clear. My surgeon says he thinks the other two should be able to come out next Friday.

I'm still dressing my wounds and wearing a compression bra. My body does not look natural. It is far from feeling natural. If I overdo it, as I have a tendency to (surprise!), my chest feels very tight and sore. Not only my chest, but under my arms as well. I never knew the vast area that breast tissue covers on the human body. It's amazing and makes a bilateral mastectomy even more uncomfortable and difficult to get used to. I did look at myself five days post-op. It took me that long to get up the nerve. After crying uncontrollably for a bit more than half an hour, I was able to carry on. I have looked again since, without tears. I am now a day shy of two weeks post-op. That's not much time to get used to something as colossal as removal of two breasts. Grace.

I know that this state of things is but for a limited time, a season. The house will get cleaned, the laundry done. My body won't always be this sore, weak, and disfigured, but it is my reality right now.

This cancer journey, which began for us at the start of 2015, has been such a journey of growth and self-discovery. It's been happy-sad, a time of deepened relationships, and a new way of looking at people and situations. In this time, I have learned so much of life is about perspective, about where your focus is, where you look. Attitude. I knew this before, but it means so much more to me now.

It's become very important to me to find balance in every circumstance. I must acknowledge the mess, but also recognize the miracles therein. That is balance. That is grace. To approach life in this way brings peace.

I'm happy to report that in the course of this last week, in the midst of tears, grief, and physical pain, I have had wonderful news from my oncology surgeon. The pathology report (testing of all breast tissue and lymph nodes removed) showed no evidence of cancer! They call this a "complete chemotherapy response." I call it a miracle. My doctor was beyond excited to relay this to me. And I am beyond relieved to relay it here now.

As I acknowledge all of the beauty, meaning, and miracles found in some of my most difficult days, I look forward to the future. I will be resuming treatment at The Block Center on Tuesday. I will receive Herceptin by IV once every three weeks for the next year. This is a targeted therapy, not a chemotherapy drug. It does have some negative side effects, which include: muscle and joint soreness; neuropathy; and heart damage. I will be working closely with my new oncology cardiologist (my newest team member, and a delightful human being, Dr. DeCara) to ensure that my heart can safely manage the regimen.

I will have another surgery in the next several months, but for now the focus will be healing from this surgery and resuming this targeted treatment. I thank God for all that I've come through and anticipate there will be much more to be thankful for in the days to come.

My husband spent the day doing laundry, wrestling with our boys, mowing the lawn, and washing doors (a project I wanted to do but physically could not). He was acting as my arms/ hands. A friend bought over dinner. We have had dinner non-stop since the day I came home from the hospital...it has been amazing. My parents have been keeping the rooms picked up, as each boy tends to leave a trail. Cindy drove me to my first haircut (a trim around the ears, really).

There is much about my life that is messy right now and much about my life that is miraculous. One of my favorite quotes is by Albert Einstein who said, "There are two ways to live your life: One is as though nothing is a miracle. The other is as though everything is a miracle." I choose to maintain balance and experience peace by recognizing the miracles in the mess.

10/4/15
There are Worse Things in the World

I was preparing to take a shower the other day and it was nothing short of a fiasco. With the wounds that were dressed across my chest, the drainage tubes that were stitched into either side of my body, and my limited mobility, it was quite a production. I had to strategize the process before executing it. It sounds dramatic, doesn't it? (I'm not trying to be melodramatic, it's just important to share what my physical situation and mind-set were at that moment.)

Once I finally made it into the shower (drainage tubes tied around my waist) I became aware of my annoyance and even anger at the state of things. I knew I was in need of an attitude adjustment. "There are worse things in the world," I reminded myself out loud.

I was enjoying the warm water and knew the situation would be much worse without warm water. Or without water altogether! There are worse things in the world than healing from what could potentially have been a life-saving surgery in a nice warm shower."Like being homeless." That would be worse. Then my thoughts went to Syria and from there to all of the refugees of the world. All the nomads risking life and limb, displaced by war or illness or poverty, giving up everything in search of a better life for their families.

I've been considering this a lot as I encounter new challenges. This Friday, I had to have a few things done in an outpatient surgical setting. I was nervous but had no idea what all was in store for me. I knew that I would be awake for the procedure and that my surgeon would be reopening one of the incisions because it was not healing properly. (Yikes...)

I arrived at the surgical center with my mom, who was immediately mistaken as my friend. *Compliment to you, Mrs. Fenlon!* I was quickly taken back to be prepared for the procedure. I had to get into a hospital gown and those fancy hospital socks, have my vital signs taken and blood sugar tested. I met with my reconstructive surgeon and introduced him to my mom. I was so glad they were able to meet. He confirmed I would be getting my drains out before the procedure, that I would be awake the whole time but that the area would be numbed so I "shouldn't feel a thing." Everything went smoothly and I was actually on my way into the operating room on time.

Once in the freezing cold room, I was transferred to the operating table, my arms put out to my sides and they began to prep for the surgery. It was similar to prepping for a C-section except I knew I wouldn't be leaving with a baby, so had a lot less excitement about the whole thing. Thankfully, my chest was still numb from the mastectomy not three weeks prior so I did not feel the shot with the local anesthetic.

It was then time to remove the drains. I was so thankful when Dr. Pavone had confirmed that I would be getting the tubes out that day. I had had a third drain but it was removed just five days after surgery. When it was removed, I was in the doctor's office, a PA removed it, and I couldn't feel a thing except relief. This time it was not to be so. They removed the drain from the left side first. "S**T!!!"

My friend Missy said it best: "It felt like the drains had healed into my chest wall and when they pulled them out it was like ripping my chest on the inside." Indeed, Missy, indeed.

The surgeon apologized profusely and the nurses sympathized. I just swore again through tears and struggled with the shock and trauma of the moment. "You can hit me if you need to," my doctor said, positioning himself on my right side ready to take the other drain out.

"No, I'll just cry," was my response. "I need a minute."

We all reasoned that perhaps the next one wouldn't hurt quite so much since the right side was numbed by the local anesthetic. With a flourish of plastic tubing, curses, and tears, the thing was out.

"Dear Heavenly Father," was all I could say through the tears as I held my chest trying to soothe myself and cool the wounded area. I never felt any such pain upon waking up from a double mastectomy. The pain of the drain removal was infinitely more intense than any I'd experienced thus far, and it was over. Just a pang of residual pain remained.

It was now time to prep for the surgery, the whole point of my visit. I was shaking uncontrollably by this point, a mix of the 64° temperature and the physical trauma. The nurses confirmed this and they weighted me down with warmed blankets, soothing me with quiet conversation.

We talked about kids and labor, men and women, parenting and so on as they put up the barrier so I couldn't see the surgical procedure, doused me with iodine and made sure I was numbed. This process was so much like a Caesarean: the drape, the numbing, feeling the pressure of the cutting, but not the sharpness of it.

I talked about my work in private practice and home care. I specifically talked about teaching coping skills to deal with anxiety and how I myself have struggled with anxiety. The nurses asked if I use the techniques myself and I had to admit I didn't use them as much as I should. All conversation was used not only to pass the time but also as a method of diverting my attention from the task at hand. It was the longest twenty minutes of my life. I could feel every pull of the stitch when he was closing the wound and asked Dr. Pavone if that meant he was about done. He was. Soon I was bandaged up, scooting myself onto the gurney, and being wheeled to the recovery waiting area. They fed me crackers and gave me water. They checked my vital signs and helped me out of bed into a chair. Truly, I was feeling fine but let them proceed with their jobs. When my clothing was finally returned to me, I wasted no time in getting dressed and ready to go. My mom was brought back in time to hear the discharge instructions and to collect me. Then we were off.

As I've reflected on the events of that day just two days ago, I'm so happy to say it is done. The incision looks much better than the previous one and I am thankful for a caring and skilled surgeon who has taken very good care of me. My lift restrictions remain: nothing over ten pounds and I have to watch the pushing/pulling. I know that truly there are worse things in the world than what I had to deal with when taking a shower with drainage tubes or even going through painful procedures.

So much of life is about perspective. I'm learning to balance my experiences by acknowledging the pain but also recognizing the miracles and precious moments in the midst of it. I want to remember, no matter what I'm facing, that there are worse things in the world. With this mindset, I hope, comes clarity as well as compassion; clarity, to always keep an even perspective about a situation; compassion, to always remember to reach out and recognize the pain and struggle of others.

There are worse things in the world than what I am experiencing right now and maybe the next person I meet is living that reality. I want to be clear- minded and sensitive so as not to miss an opportunity to lift someone up.

10/5/15
Something for My Children

I entered a contest on Facebook at the end of August. It was on the NBC 5 Chicago Facebook page and they were looking for cancer survivors who wanted to share their story of survivorship and how they are "giving back."

At first I was wary. I've been down a similar road before and was hurt by it. In a time of need, my family and I had shared our story, accepted help (financial, in-kind, emotional, spiritual, anything we could get...it was a time of *need*!) and had received criticism and even judgment for it.

It was the days of snail mail. I didn't even have an email address at that time. There was no Facebook (Mark Zuckerberg was only eight years old), no texting, no face time, just simple letters written on paper. Easy enough to slip an anonymous letter into an envelope with no return address and tell a seventeen-year-old cancer patient that she shouldn't be "begging for money." After that, my parents began screening my mail.

There were many blessings and much encouragement and

love during that time as well. Family, friends, and church-family surrounded us, and our tiny town in northern Michigan absolutely opened its heart, efforts, and finances on our behalf. Cheboygan, Michigan; Cornerstone Chapel (now River of Life Church); Cheboygan Area High School; and the Fenlon, Fisher, Goebel and Aldrich clans all rallied to give support to my family in a time of deficit and depletion.

When I was diagnosed with Her2+ breast cancer in February of this year, I was faced again with a decision: to share my story openly or to be quiet about it. It didn't take but a minute to decide to go all in on disclosing details about this cancer journey (despite the response). It was a way to make meaning of a situation that would otherwise seem like one of meaningless pain. Not only did I find blogging to be extremely therapeutic, but I also found that as I shared my story and people responded with "thank you," "that was so encouraging," and "your words are so inspiring" that I wanted to explain more. I knew that I had made the right choice. Not only do I want to share my story to encourage and inspire others but also to leave something lasting for my children.

At ages seventeen and eighteen, I lived with my parents, wrote in a journal, and told them every day that I loved them. At age forty-one, I live with my husband and four little boys. I tell them I love them on a daily basis and try to live and behave in such a way that would communicate that love and to teach them how to deal with circumstances in life with a positive attitude. And I write a blog. I write to sort things out in my head but also to share the wisdom gained and lessons learned in the midst of a difficult situation. I like the permanence and transparency of online journaling. My boys will be able to access my feelings, thoughts, frustrations, and breakthroughs for as long as they live (probably).

And now this: I was chosen by NBC 5 to be one of the cancer survivors they featured for the month of October as they teamed up with Lexus to salute survivors. My parents, Cindy, the boys, and I spent a relaxing afternoon at Perry Farm Park with Gina, Dave, and Sherene from NBC 5. The members of the NBC crew were friendly, creative, and calm. It was easy to spend a laid-back few hours with them and to share our story.

I've always felt that television, video, and film are eternal. The idea of video journaling messages to loved ones has always been inspiring to me. Now I have a thirty-second video journal which serves as a little something for my children. When I am not longer on this earth and they remain, they will remember. At ages five, four, four, and two, there is not much of this cancer experience that they fully comprehend. They are intuitive and sensitive, but the details and depth of the situation is not completely understood. (Rightfully so.) But they are a part of this story; they play a major role in every thought, movement, and decision my husband and I make. So, this thirty-second video clip is a little something for them. It commemorates our journey through cancer together. The video clip can be seen on my website at: www.sarahfenlonfalk.com or on the NBC 5

Chicago website, search under Sarah Fenlon Falk.

10/13/15
About Breasts

I have to admit I've been noticing breasts lately. It's the strangest thing. I've caught myself in the midst of people watching, all of a sudden wondering if the woman who is bouncing through the parking lot has real breasts or implants. Sometimes the thoughts continue and I wonder if those breasts are real, how well that individual takes care of those real breasts, knowing full well they aren't something to be taken for granted!

There have been times that I've actually felt sorry for some women's breasts as they are squeezed and lifted to unnatural heights for the sake of effect. It looks uncomfortable and I wonder how healthy this could possibly be to strangle one's breasts for hours a day. However, I've also recognized that overly bouncy women may not be offering much (if any) support to their ladies, which can't be good either.

I have sat and watched and wondered which woman in a crowd at the mall is a breast cancer survivor or which woman at the restaurant will find out in the near future that she has breast cancer. As for me, there are moments when I still cannot believe that this has happened/is happening to me. So, I sit and look at breasts. I've been told it is all part of the process of grief and healing. I've been told, "It's natural," though, I'm not sure I've heard anyone speak much about "breast watching". But I will. I will tell you all about it.

I live vicariously through the nursing mother and remember when I fed my babies in that beautiful, intimate way. The reminder of this blessing causes me to be grateful that my breasts had been intact and were able to perform one of the tasks they were created for.

I envy the young, healthy bodies I see, their uncut legs, bellies, and breasts. I cannot imagine what I might look like or what I might be doing had I not experienced cancer the first time and could walk or run about on two healthy legs. It's inconceivable to think of what a whole, unscarred belly would look like on me. I know that I would never take back the blessing of my four boys to find out! And finally, I consider the lumps on my chest that are a man-made recreation of breasts in process, a body under construction. I find myself struggling to remember, after three short weeks, what it was like when my breasts were real, whole.

While walking outside today I could feel the tightness in my chest and under my arms and tried to maintain proper posture in the midst of it. I realized anew that my body would never be the same again. That reality is a source of grief for me. It will require time and space to adjust. I must become acquainted with this new aspect of an older body.

Yes, I have found myself looking at women and their beautiful bodies, wondering about cancer, their health and history. I've been looking at my own body as well these days and considering its history. I acknowledge the wounds, scars, and inward battles and bless my body for carrying me through so much. I am grateful for the days, years, and specific moments I have lived in this body and look forward to many more. It is a time of transition and sadness but also one of healing. I can only imagine that through this healing, and in time, I will think less about breasts.

10/18/15
The Power of "Yes"
(To Cause Me Great Anxiety)

I contemplated other titles here but settled on "The Power of 'Yes' (To Cause Me Great Anxiety)" because I believe it was after a series of "Yeses" that the anxiety began to mount. The "yes" spoken to a coworker to help on a project seemed simple enough. Not much would be required of me. There would be minimum time commitment, little planning or effort. But I couldn't just set about the task of preparing the way I usually do.

And then there was the "yes" I spoke to the friend at church. Again, there would be minimal time requirement and minimal effort on my part. Both "yeses" were spoken for things I typically enjoy and like to do: public speaking and music. I had agreed to help, in both cases, without hesitation. After all, I'm feeling better and it is about time I start getting back into the groove of things. (Right?)

I've been down the road of anxiety and panic before. It's

not new to me, and I can recognize the signs. One of the most difficult parts about anxiety for me is that though I may be physically capable, and even if it's something I love (or maybe people I enjoy spending time with) the feelings of fear or stress can (and often do) so easily trump the positives. It's at that point I become depressed because I don't feel like "myself" and if I'm not careful, I can become an anxious, sad, angry mess.

It wasn't until I had the nightmare this week that I realized perhaps I was anxious about something. Monday night I had a dream. I dreamed I was in an old building. It actually looked like an old school building, the kind that has the very hard floors, fluorescent lighting, and smells as though there must be asbestos in the ceiling and walls. I went from the bottom floor to the top and was looking for something or someone. It was dusk and I was very agitated, though I did not know why.

Once on the second floor, I found myself in an apartment. There were a few lamps on but otherwise it was quickly getting dark and it was hard to see the details of each room. I kept looking around for that someone or something, and realized that at one end of the apartment there was a fire. It took a moment to register what I was seeing, but once I had a grip on the fact that the room was on fire, I began a frantic search for a fire extinguisher and could not find one. I decided to double back and get out, since there was no extinguisher to try to fend the flames off. I turned around to run away from the flames and found there was a fire on the other end of the apartment as well. There was no escape. I was trapped. There were no windows, no doors, just a dimly lit room with flames destroying the place on either side of me.

I woke up panicked, and as so often happens with disturbing and vivid dreams, it took me some time to shake it off. Throughout the morning as I was working to recover from what my mind had experienced in the night, I began to consider if the dream held any significance and if so, what. Immediately I began to think about what is happening in my life at this moment. Just the day before, we had begun talks, negotiations for releasing our captive worker, my mom (aka Mimi). She has been at our home since my surgery to help with the kids, chores, and just to be available so that I have a better chance of sticking to my lift restrictions while healing. I will be returning to work in a week and it was suggested that perhaps Mimi would like to be able to return to her home and her own work there.

The truth is, I am feeling better and am able to do much by myself already. My doctor will release me for work on Friday. Despite all of this, I'm not looking forward to seeing my mom go. It's been a great support having her here and thinking of her going (far) away is difficult for me.

Then there's the idea of returning to work. It's not the physical capabilities that concern me as much as the emotional requirements involved; the emotional task of leaving the comfort and safety of my home where I have been resting, working to heal, and have been a constant in my kids' lives for five weeks now. I'm starting to feel the tension and anxiety much as I did years ago when I suffered from panic attacks and intense anxiety.

Not only having my mom planning to leave, my plans to return to work, and adding a couple extra tasks to the mix, but also with all of this are the continued doctor appointments, and continued treatment.

We are in the process of planning yet another surgery for this year; consequently, my mind is preoccupied. I have pulled out the tried and true methods of dealing with anxiety. I have been practicing deep breathing, relaxation, and meditation. I have been reading for pleasure and playing my guitar (something I missed much when I was unable to hold anything near my chest). And of course I am certain to write whatever needs letting out of this head of mine. I've also been looking into other techniques for healing and anxiety-management, yoga poses specifically for breast cancer and anxiety, and watching documentaries on health and wellness.

I received a text from my coworker today and it took the edge off. The gist of it was this: due to confusion and miscommunication, the project was done and my assistance would no longer be needed. While some part of me had truly been looking forward to it (as explained at length above) I admit I did feel weight lift from my shoulders.

I have received no such reprieve regarding the other commitment I have made, but as I know what to do when anxiety attempts to rule my life, I will carry on, and when all is said and done, I'm sure I will have enjoyed myself and will be thankful for having the skills to cope with the overwhelming emotions.

I'm reminded by this nightmare, by the feelings of tension, by the sensation of oncoming panic, to listen to my body and to attend to its message. I will honor my body by caring for it and by resting my mind. "Yes" is a beautiful word and should carry with it no anxiety for me when used wisely. Therefore my "yes" will remain in reserve for the time being.

10/27/15
And This Was Going to Be the Funny One

After church on Sunday, it was suggested that I read the blog by Jason Micheli, who is a United Methodist minister in Virginia. He is also a cancer patient and blogs about his experiences. I did read bits of his blog and laughed at what Jason had to say. His levity in the midst of pastoring, parenting, and cancer treatment lifted my spirits and reminded me of my own sense of humor...somewhere. Out. There.

I remember the days of inpatient chemotherapy as a seventeen-year-old girl, answering all of the intake questions with the most ridiculous or snarky answers I could think of. Such as:

Form question: Sex _____.

My answer: Not at this time.

Form question: Any special toileting or bathroom needs?

My answer: Toilet, toilet paper, sink, soap, that'll do it.

While it's not very funny when I read it now in the comfort of home, it was stinking hilarious when I was filling out the paperwork for the hundredth time, anxious about getting sick (again), and sad that I wasn't home or in school enjoying my senior year of high school. Anything I could do to be silly or funny (in my way) I did, for my own sanity and for the sake of those around me.

This go-round with cancer has been different. I don't joke about many things. I find my mind muddled and I'm forced to pick through thoughts, feelings, and tasks in a way that I've not had to before. I'm teaching myself to acknowledge my own pain and to offer others the freedom to confess their pain as well. I have found myself downplaying where I am at during any given moment and have witnessed others belittling their struggle because they don't think it measures up to my own. Not so. Life experience, trouble, pain, it's all relative, isn't it?

So, the other day I found myself being funny. I was telling a coworker about the rocks I have in my chest. They are not actually rocks; they are saline- filled silicone expanders that are stretching my muscle and skin to a shape where eventually I will have implants placed so that I will look like I have breasts. (They just feel like rocks.) I laughed as I talked about feeling like I am being weighed down and could walk bent over, ha ha, and how if I were dropped in the water I'd definitely sink, ha ha ha. I walked away and thought I was going to bawl. I meant what I said, and it was funny at that moment, but the truth of it is, feeling like I have rocks in my chest, and knowing the breasts I was born with are gone, made me so sad in the very next moment.

I had started composing this post in my mind on Sunday and smiled and laughed. *"Finally, some comedy,"* I had thought. *"I remember this girl!"* Monday flew by, Tuesday's return to work went long but better than anticipated, and today was cold and rainy to match my mood. By the time I sat down to write, I was in tears. *"This was supposed to be the funny one,"* was the only thing I could think as I sat down to pour out my heart without humor.

So, I have done what I would recommend to any friend of mine going through the same: I have followed Jason Micheli on Twitter, pulled out the funniest and most helpful book I have found about breast cancer (*100 Perks of Having Cancer plus 100 Health Tips for Surviving It* by Florence Strang, M.Ed. and Susan Gonzalez, B.S.N.) and have listened to some of my favorite music. Last, but probably most important, I have sat down to write. I have *needed* to write about this experience like I've never needed to write before. In the same way that a body feels hunger, I feel the need to put all that I am into words. Sometimes I feel my words are inadequate, but I always feel better after getting them out.

While this may not be a funny post, it has been therapeutic for me, and as always, it is my hope that it will ring true for someone who perhaps couldn't find his or her own words. It is clear to me I have not lost my sense of humor by any means; I am just coping differently this time around. A special thanks to Jason Micheli for the laughs.

11/1/15
More Than Breasts

I've been all mixed up lately. To say that I have ups and downs would be a fair statement, except it sounds too casual. The space of time between the ups and the downs could be simply a matter of minutes. My mind is like a runaway train. I can't keep up. It's like trying to talk to a four-year-old who has just eaten some of his Halloween candy, is up an hour past his bedtime, and has a new movie playing on the television within eye- and earshot. Try as you might, you cannot get that little boy to make eye contact with you. There is nothing you can say or do that will make him avert his eyes from the TV, help him to stand still, or keep him quiet. (I know, I've tried it!) And this is the perfect illustration for how my brain is behaving these days. I'm All. Over. The. Place.

While I'm scattered, muddled, and easily distracted, there are some issues I can count on to harass me daily, self-esteem being one of them. My self-esteem is in the tank (most minutes). Pete has found I cannot take a joke if it is directed at me, my looks, my performance, my words, anything about me. I have zero tolerance for the kidding and have just slightly more for constructive criticism. Overall, it's getting better, slowly but surely, due to much effort on my part.

I can be a comparer, one who compares. I think that's one of the reasons I've always struggled with self-esteem, because when you're looking for it everyone else appears smarter, prettier, more talented, happier, wealthier, healthier, kinder, and put together. Of course I'm not the only one with a mask to wear, but when I'm in my weighing and measuring mood, I forget that and assume those aren't masks I'm seeing. So lately, there's been a lot of that going on. I have had instances when I needed to remind myself not to compare and could easily move on. Not so these days. No sir, no ma'am. Not so. Truly, it's been a long time since I've had issues with comparing and it is perplexing to think that I am dealing with it now.

And beyond comparing, I've been critical. Criticism is not a new struggle in my life either. Disapproval and I go way back. But since being reintroduced, she has proven to be much more harsh than I remember. Never have I picked myself apart the way I am doing these days, inside and out. My parenting, profession, marriage, mind, and body are all on the chopping block without hesitation. I've caught myself in a moment and have rescued a shred of dignity in the midst of ripping my body to pieces. A lot of this censure is focused on my body. But then, a lot of focus has been on my body this year out of necessity. The sad thing is, before I was diagnosed with breast cancer in February 2015, I was very happy with my body. This amazing body has survived cancer once before, sustained the assault of yearlong chemotherapy treatments, endured an extensive bone-drilling surgery to place titanium rods in the femur and tibia, and to replace the knee joint when the tumor was removed. This body has carried four babies—two of them at the same time. My former breasts fed all four babies for ten to twelve months each. In February of 2015, I was in awe of the body that preformed such feats. I didn't mind the extra skin from the twin pregnancy. It was easy to ignore the infrequent dizzy spells and difficulty breathing from the hernia that pregnancy produced. I didn't mind that gravity's work was apparent in many areas. None of that mattered. I was healthy, active, and strong. This mama bear could do pretty well to keep up with the four little cubs. That was eight months ago.

I've noticed in the past few weeks how I'm looking at other women's breasts, which I've been told is normal after a mastectomy, but it's more than just breasts: I'm looking at their flat tummies, strong arms and legs, long hair. I was determined to keep my hair short and not to dye it, but now I wish my hair would grow faster and have wondered if there are "natural" hair-dying products out there. I shake my head as I think about some of the negative things I've had to say about myself lately. And the crazy thing is I have a husband who is utterly attracted to me no matter what I look like and he tells me as much, often. How can my self-esteem be suffering so when I have all of these miracles and affirmations in my life as confirmation of my value and purpose? But I am having trouble here. It's beyond me.

Being inside the comparing and criticisms of a muddled brain isn't the most pleasant place to be. But even as I may, at times, allow my mind to wander into thoughts of "who has it better than me," I put my proverbial foot down and remind myself of the suffering all around me. I remember to pray for those who are in pain, sick, and hurting more than I can imagine. They are champions of strength, perseverance, and grace. Putting my situation in perspective by considering others always helps straighten me out.

12/1/15
Filter, Balance, Breathe

In my quest to learn and formulate a strategy for health and disease prevention, I have become overwhelmed with information. Not only that, but as I share what I'm reading and learning, I have come to realize that this is becoming overwhelming for some of my friends and family. Especially in the area of nutrition, there are so many ideas out there as to what is the best way to feed the body. If you look at the bookstore or do an online search for "diet," "nutrition," or the like, you will find many differing opinions. There are articles on topics that go beyond simply what to eat and offer weight-loss and health solutions regarding how often, when, and how to eat. (Paying attention to your food does assist in digestion, so I'm not knocking the "how" here; I'm just proving the point that all this information can be overwhelming!)

I'm sorry if you've become confused or overwhelmed with me in this process! If you have, I'd like to share what I've learned to do throughout my search. With all of this information I have two choices: to **filter it** or **file it**. If a particular article or topic seems a little far-fetched to me from the get-go, I will filter that one. But, if I read a book or a study that makes a lot of sense to me intuitively and provides practical tips for real life, then I will most certainly file it. So, just remember as you're trying to sort through all of my posts, Facebook shares, and tweets that if the information does not seem to fit into your mindset or lifestyle, keep what you can from the info and let the rest go. Filter or file it.

The next point I want to be sure to make about this info overload is the idea of balance. Balance the time you spend reading or looking into health and wellness issues. Sometimes too much information is simply that: too much information. I've begun to realize I really need to put a cap on how much time I allow myself to spend searching or reading about prevention and wellness, even though that is my crusade at the moment. If I spend too much time on this, I am neglecting those things in my life that are necessary for my health such as solitude, quality time with my family and friends, time for creativity, and so on. I don't want to be up in my head all the time, with my nose in a book or eyes glued to a computer screen. I need to feel the sun on my face, move around a bit, and listen to the stories and laughter of my children.

What I have found in this process is that I have produced stress within myself by overanalyzing food, wellness, and prevention. This has begun to outweigh the good of the information I've been gathering. I've taken steps toward establishing boundaries though the "filter it/file it" system and then by remembering to seek a balance in my life. But it is time for me to take boundaries a step further with myself in regards to the information overload. I must step back and evaluate what I do know, then move ahead. I'm fighting right now and I need to take a moment to breathe and remind myself to float.

12/6/15
Behind, Ahead, and Sometime in Between

The weather has changed from my beloved sunny days to the rainy, snowy, chilled ones. It's not an easy transition for me. It affects my mood and energy level. It certainly affects my knee—I have had more pain in my knee in the last few weeks than I've had in a long time. The pain in my knee is more than what I experienced after the bilateral mastectomy in September. It's like adding insult to injury. Only I consider the knee the injury and the mastectomy the insult.

I remember during my first cancer experience, one of my most difficult struggles was feeling left out, even though most of the community knew of my story and subsequently knew me at the time. I wasn't able to attend school regularly, I missed out on a lot of social events and relationships that year, and I had to grieve the loss of that part of my life.

Even with the struggles, bone cancer wasn't as demeaning as breast cancer can sometimes seem. With breast cancer, there's always a touch of awkwardness when talking about surgery and the reconstruction process. A part of the body that was once intimate conversation between husband and wife has now become a topic in conversation with many. The discussion, my breasts, always seems to make me feel like I have to help the other person not feel uncomfortable even though they were asking about my health in regard to cancer, in regard to my breasts. Then there's always the eye contact and it seems both of us in conversation work to avoid looking down. I talk with my hands a lot, so when I'm discussing the surgeries and reconstruction I try to remember to keep my hands in my lap, not to demonstrate around my breasts or draw any more attention to the area than necessary. When my knee was the center of attention, I never felt uncomfortable. A knee is a knee after all.

I do appreciate the concern and support that is expressed time and again through questions and conversation and have become quite comfortable in my response. I've never been a shy or closed person, so this was not a big step for me to make, becoming comfortable with a conversation about my body and my health.

As I sit bundled up on this cold winter's evening, I'm pondering the year's end, which will come in just a few short weeks. In that time, we are hoping that I will be able to schedule my final reconstructive surgery. In the next few weeks, I will also be scheduling an ultrasound of my knee to see what this little mass is that's growing out of my leg just below the kneecap. An MRI had been scheduled for my knee; however, the tissue expanders that are in place for the reconstruction of my breasts contain metal, something we didn't remember or realize until I was being placed into the MRI and my chest started caving in. All is well. Everything went back to where it was supposed to be once I was brought out and away from the machine. Live and learn, I guess. So, no MRI for my knee; we will be waiting to see if an ultrasound can give us more helpful information than the X-rays did. The mass didn't show up on the X- ray. While the pain in my knee has receded and I am able to walk fairly well again, that little bump continues to grow.

While we wait for surgery, ultrasound, and answers, I will be having Herceptin treatment on Wednesday, and if I'm to stay on track that will mean I will be having treatment again on the 30th, just two days before the new year. A new year. I am amazed at where I have been this year; it almost scares me to look back at it. So instead of thinking back, I slide down deeper under the covers, pull my cozy hat down over my ears, rearrange the pillow under my knee, and think ahead.

12/19/15
Surprise Surgery and Other Adventures

Last Friday evening around 4:30 p.m., I received a call from my surgeon's office stating they had one opening for surgery in 2015, Thursday afternoon, December 17. This frustrated me because we had bought advance tickets to see *Star Wars: The Force Awakens*, which we have been looking forward to for months. But besides the first-world inconvenience of having to schedule surgery around *going to the movies*, I was worried. If I were to have surgery on Thursday, I had less than a week to prepare. Would I be able to get all the pieces in place before then? Would my parents be able to alter their schedule to be here? Would I be able to get Christmas errands done in advance of the surgery?

Beyond the concerns of planning and scheduling the surgery on such short notice, I have to admit I've been struggling with anxiety again. I'd spent days crying on and off throughout the day for reasons unknown. I'd kiss my boys goodbye before leaving for work or a doctor's appointment and randomly wonder if this would be the last time I would be kissing them, holding them. I've dealt with nightmares of a post-operative disfigured body that I couldn't bear to look at even in my dreams. These emotions, thoughts, and feelings alone left me exhausted and spent.

I did schedule the surgery. I did have the surgery on Thursday, December 17. This surgery was to complete the post-mastectomy reconstruction. Again, I must go through the process of getting used to the way I look. There have been so many changes to my body in the last several months that it's been hard to keep up.

My parents were able to come the day before and stay with the boys while my husband took me for surgery. Amazingly enough, the surgery was outpatient. Knowing that it was an outpatient "procedure" made it feel like less of a big deal when considering it. The pain I feel in my body today, however, reminds me that it was still surgery and nothing to take lightly. I have stayed down much of the day today, making up for the activity of yesterday. I didn't rest yesterday as I should have and now I pay for it.

I'm so thankful for doctors who are caring and who know what they are doing. My surgeon has such a delightful bedside manner and is so kind and patient. I felt absolutely confident in him going into the OR. It was emotionally uncomfortable (to say the least) for me to have to say goodbye to my husband, but Pete was with me until the last moment when they wheeled me away. They said they had given me some medicine to make me sleepy and as my bed rolled down the hall, I was concerned that I was still awake.

That's the last I remember. Waking up, I had a hard time swallowing from the tube having been down my throat. Pete was sitting in a chair across from me, smiling. He told me the doctor said everything had gone well. He told me I was so pretty. I tried to open my eyes fully, to wake up, but I couldn't. Pete had to dress me, help me into a wheelchair, be my eyes and ears for all discharge instructions and the like, drive me home, and put me to bed. I don't remember much about the rest of that day. I ate a poached egg before going to sleep.

The next day I decided to change my pajamas. I talked, snuggled, and sat with my boys. One of my four-year-olds, Sam, asked me to be his girlfriend. He suggested that a cracker with egg salad on it might make my knee feel better. I told him I thought he had a good idea for helping me feel better. I've been having issues with my knee, which we will now be able to look into (the tissue expanders that were removed in my surgery on Thursday were not compatible with MRI. Now that they are out, I will be able to have the MRI). This is yet another adventure to prepare for.

I had hoped that after the surgery on Thursday, I would be able to close a medical chapter in my life's book; however, it seems that will not be possible. My orthopedic surgeon does not want to waste any time in figuring out what is wrong with my knee. I have an unidentified cyst growing just beneath and to the right of my kneecap. My first cancer diagnosis in 1991 was osteogenic sarcoma, bone cancer, of the left femur. Because this cyst is in the region of my first cancer, the doctors are remaining cautious.

And so, as I rest and recover from this surgery, I am planning an MRI next week to determine what this growth on my left leg may be. I brace myself for more answers I may not want to hear. But I always remember these words and try to live by them: "Jesus said, 'Let not your heart be troubled. Trust in God, trust also in me... Peace I leave with you; my peace I give you... Do not let your hearts be troubled and do not be afraid.'" John 14:1, 27.

I believe that every problem has a provision attached to it. So I will rest, watch, and wait. I receive peace and remind myself there is no need to fear. I look forward to yet another adventure, much like a last-minute surgery, where I will be witness to Provision and Purpose in my life.

***Note: after this was written I was able to have an MRI on my knee and it was found to be a good old-fashioned cyst, benign. Good news to ring in the New Year!

12/29/15
I Never Thought THIS Would Be the Struggle

At this point in the breast cancer experience, after all the diagnostic testing, subsequent diagnosis, decision-making regarding treatment, subsequent chemotherapy treatment, sickness, weight loss, weight gain, time off work, working while unwell, time in bed, decision-making regarding surgeries, subsequent surgeries, family upheaval, countless doctor appointments, laughter and tears, that *this* would be the struggle kind of baffles me.

I was talking to my friend Amanda the other day. (She also happens to be a fellow breast cancer survivor.) We were discussing how shut off we were emotionally to be able to manage almost a full year of doctors' appointments, treatments, illness, etc. Now that we are no longer in the thick of things and have some headspace and time to devote to feelings, those feelings we have pent up for months seem overwhelming to us. The dam has broken and has flooded my mental space, my emotions, my very soul. Torrents of emotions are not the only seas to navigate, but this new body as well. After so many physical changes over the past several months I feel like an alien in my own body. Amanda said that if she hears that she just "needs time to get used to the new normal" one more time, she may lose it. I get that. And I had to laugh because I've used that very statement in sessions with my clients, with family members and caregivers of patients, and in personal pep talks.

Here's the thing about the new normal: it's strange. It's all foreign. I happened to like the "old" body I had. It wasn't picture perfect but it was all mine. I knew it well and over time had cultivated a very healthy and appreciative relationship with it, every bit of it. Now, I struggle with self-hate. It may sound extreme but I must be honest.

My task right now is to constantly remind myself that this body did not ask for cancer, it did not ask for surgery or changes. This body is still "my body," just in different feeling and form. It will take time to develop a relationship with this new body. In the process, it will do no good to deny the feelings I am experiencing. So I must learn to acknowledge the pain of my emotions as well as the pain I am experiencing in body, to nurture my body while caring for my emotional self. While they may seem to be in conflict, the work will be to assimilate, to blend body and spirit. They seem to be at odds right now. However, I remind myself that I do not "hate" this body. This body has survived a number of traumatic events in 2015. This body has carried me through.

I want to nurture and care for this frame I have been gifted with. It is glorious.

I want to acknowledge all that I feel in my spirit at this time as well: the grief, the anger, the confusion. In doing so, I hope to rally both body and spirit to the same purpose—to heal. I never thought *this* would be the struggle at this point. I am thankful for every new day, each moment, to be with my family, to watch my children grow. However, I do feel the expectation is that I would be giddy with excitement over being "done." But I need you to know: I am *not* done. In some ways, the most difficult piece of healing is beginning now. I can handle tasks and to-dos much better than I can handle inner conflict, insecurity, and sadness. This time of "reconstruction" is about much more than my breasts. I'm learning to love and accept myself again, the way I look and feel now. I'm sorting through the events and emotions of the last several months. It is a busy time internally and will require time and space. I'm grateful for the support, prayers, words of encouragement, and for every single person in my life. Because you are in my life, you need to know: I'm not done, I am just beginning.

Journal entry, December 14, 1996:

One thing I've realized that has been very difficult for me
to deal with is the issue of my identity. It's hard enough to
figure out who you are and where you're going in life
without having something throw you off course the way
cancer does.

When I had cancer, I was "Sarah Fenlon, the girl with
cancer." My whole town knew me as that. I was in the
paper, interviewed on television, and the reason for many
of the area fundraisers. People would say "hi" to me and
I often didn't know who they were, but they knew me.
Many people helped my family financially and also
provided meals for my father and three siblings who were
left at home while my mom and I were in the hospital. I
knew who I was then: Sarah Fenlon, the girl with cancer.
I also had a solitary purpose and goal during this time: to
fight and stay alive!

When my chemotherapy was finished and I had my
"end of chemo" celebration, visits and phone calls
dwindled fast. Once my hair grew to a healthy-looking
length and the visible traces of my life with cancer were
gone, my identity also seemed to be gone. With the
exception of a few scars and many memories, "Sarah
Fenlon the girl with cancer" was no more. The fight I had
been waging was over and I was at a loss as to what
should come next. I had to deal with the question, "Who
is Sarah Fenlon aside from cancer?" I was not the same

girl I had been before I was diagnosed. I was not only older in age but about ten years older in life experience.

Unfortunately, I do not have a "Five Step Plan to Gaining Identity;" however, I have learned there is more to life than hairstyles and guys. There's even more than the things that had so consumed me before, such as soccer and band. I had to realize that life is precious. I was created and am here on this earth for a specific purpose. Through my illness, I came to know the God of Creation more intimately. I relied on His strength to get me through the loneliest of times. It was through knowledge of His love for me as well as the purpose He has for me, that gave me courage. I knew that even if I died, everything would be all right, but since I have lived, I know there is something more I am needed for.

Now, I want to share this hope and strength. I have an identity; I know who I am aside from cancer. It's not something I could write on paper; it's a peace in my heart. A peace that is there because I'm trying to find what God wants me to do now. As I seek Him and as He leads me, my identity is reaffirmed through Him; my significance is reestablished.

EPILOGUE

4/30/2017
The Real Me

It's difficult to summarize what's been going on in my life, heart, and mind lately. As I am home recovering from my most recent breast reconstruction surgery, the thought strikes me that I didn't share this decision with many people. This was a surgery scheduled back in January for April 19, 2017 and yet very few people knew about it. It has been profound in many ways and I will try to share the decision-making process, the surgical experience, as well as recovery, in a way that encapsulates the breadth and depth of all that has happened to me throughout. *It's huge.*

I had a tearful discussion with my new plastic surgeon in January. I had met him after seeking a second opinion regarding the current state of my reconstruction. I shared with him how I disliked the implants that had replaced my breast tissue after my bilateral mastectomy September 14, 2015. In fact, I had been through three different sets of implants in attempt to find a more natural fit and feel, but to no avail. They felt cold and hard. *I* felt fake. Having implants was very counterintuitive for me as I try to live very simply and naturally. Since chemo, I had even forsaken wearing daily makeup for the sake of skin health and living more organically. So I could never settle into the implants and was not able to move forward with nipple reconstruction. The talk returned to my original wish, for a DIEP flap procedure. The flap procedure requires tissue, fat, and veins taken from one target area and transplanted the chest area to reconstruct breasts. This results in living, warm, and soft tissue. I had been told previously that I didn't have enough fat/tissue anywhere else to transplant and create two breasts. All along, I had accepted that it was impossible for me yet still wished there were some way to have the procedure done.

That day in January my plastic surgeon, Dr. Fine, was so patient and supportive. I knew he was with me throughout that conversation and in the midst of it he stated, "We can do it if that's what you want." We discussed the pros and cons of the surgery, including the fact that my body would look much different afterward due to the fact that there wasn't a lot of tissue/fat to work with. I expressed my desire for a natural feeling body and to be rid of the implants, no matter the size of the end result. Once all details were discussed and questions answered, we determined to wait until after spring break to schedule the surgery. Dr. Fine knew we had a family trip planned for spring break and he wanted me to be physically able to enjoy it, not to be recovering from major surgery. So we scheduled the procedure for April 19. I told my husband Pete about the surgery, dates, and recovery times, and then we didn't talk about it again.

The odd thing about all of this is I've been very determined to have this surgery done, to feel more natural and be rid of the implants, to have my hernia repaired and port removed all in one fell swoop. However, despite my resolve, there has been much anxiety surrounding the decision made, the surgery and healing process. I had set it aside, perhaps avoiding the thought of it so that when April 19 was just a few days away, we still hadn't solidified how we would get there, if we would spend the night before near the hospital, where we would park, etc. And even early that morning, April 19, after being checked in, IV in, and wheeled away from my husband, the last thought that went through my head was, "it's too late to stop now." And then, "Wait!" The next thing I knew, I was being carted from one area of the hospital to the next to spend the night in the ICU. They would monitor my blood flow very closely there to assure that my new vein pathways were flowing properly.

I don't want to use this time or space to belabor the physical aspects of waking up after an extensive eight-hour surgery. I do want to say that when I was finally awake in my room I realized I couldn't move my arms or legs. They were very heavy and bloated from all of the fluids being pumped through me. This caused fear and anxiety to grip me. I was lying there, helpless. Anxiety and I go way back. I have learned many coping skills through the years and utilized them all there in that hospital room. I breathed as deeply and peacefully as I could. I prayed. I turned on the TV if my thoughts became obsessive or overwhelming. But mostly, I prayed. Even after leaving the ICU and returning home four days later, anxiety still picked at me. I continued to breathe and pray. I talked to my husband, mother, and my children. I texted friends and began to move around more, sleep a bit more comfortably, and see marked physical improvements.

Anxiety doesn't want to let me off the hook. I've feared separation from my husband, my children, my parents. I've feared cancer returning to my body after all this effort. But I was gently reminded that healing is a process, to choose faith over fear, to remember and to trust in the God who holds my life in His hands. (And the lives of those I do not want to let go of). I had a great Facebook thread going with all kinds of things that my friends, my people, remember when they are in need of encouragement or strength. They shared and reminded me. Family and friends and church family have been sending cards, bouquets, love, and prayers to me in a mighty way. My husband bought me a journal and wrote something I will treasure for the rest of my life, all while he waited for me to come out of surgery. My children have made me get well cards and pictures. Anxiety has been forced into a corner. I acknowledge my fear but don't hang out with it. Fear is a waste of my time. Beyond the anxiety, physically I am making strides daily. When I came home from the hospital one week ago today, I had six drainage tubes coming out of my body. My poor children wanted to get close and snuggle (as did I!) but the first day or two we had to go slow and I found a creative way to be close while also being barricaded by pillows. It worked.

At my post-operative appointment last Wednesday, five of those six drainage tubes were removed. It was an amazing time as I had feared their removal based on a prior painful experience, only to have a positive experience this time. I gave God glory and thanked my doctor and his assistant profusely. Even though I couldn't yet stand up straight I felt a ton lighter after that. Since I don't take narcotics, I could drive as soon as I felt able and so I drove to and from that appointment. I made it into Chicago and back (about an hour each way) with no issues. I was tired but felt so accomplished that day. Every day, I walk more, move more, do more. I am not hurrying or pushing myself; I'm just stretching to see what I can do.

I feel real. No implants. The skin is warm and soft. I look a bit Frankenstein-ish, but that doesn't even bother me. That's how deep the psychological upset was for me surrounding those implants. Even though my skin's surface is reminiscent of a patchwork quilt, inside I feel free and light. I feel whole. Real. I've not allowed myself to wonder why I had to wait so long for this, why this wasn't simply the first and only surgery I had to undergo. The past is laid down. It has been quite a journey that has led me here and I am grateful. God took care of me. He gave me a gifted surgeon. He provided a supportive family and amazing friends to walk with me. There is no room for anything but gratitude and thanksgiving here. My next doctor's appointment is this week. The last drain will be removed then. I will stand straight soon. I will return to work and an active life with an active family. But it will be the real me. I feel almost as though a part of me was lost during this reconstruction process. When I had bone cancer in 1991/92, the treatment process was cut and dry. There was a start and an end point. Breast cancer has been a much different experience. I sometimes have to remind myself that all these procedures and surgeries are not to address cancer in my body. No, I am cancer-free, thank you Jesus! But instead, each step has been in effort to piece a body back together after treatment. I was diagnosed on February 11, 2015 and completed breast cancer treatment June 21, 2016. This reconstruction journey has seemed arduous and unsettling. It has seemed as though I have not been *allowed* to move past breast cancer. My foreign, unfinished body has been a constant reminder, a constant issue to contend with. Now, today, I must say I feel resolution is right around the corner. Where I could never conceive of continuing with nipple reconstruction when I had the implants, I am ready to do so now. Again, all I can say is that I have no room for anything but gratitude and thanksgiving. I feel confidence returning. I feel strength building in my limbs and my spirit. I feel like I am either returning to or finally becoming the real me, and it is glorious.

Resources

Because you may have picked up this book for information and as a resource, I want to provide a list of those things that I found most helpful to me during my cancer journey. I hope you will be encouraged, inspired, informed, and uplifted. Blessings to you, Reader.

Testimonials: *Radical Remission* by Dr. Kelly Turner, RadicalRemission.com

Encouragement on Parenting and Spirituality: LisajoBaker.com

Spirituality: Renovare.com; Renovare podcast on iTunes

Nutrition and Wellness: KelliBonomo.com

Heart Health information: American Heart Association at www.heart.org/HEARTORG/

Mental/Emotional/Spiritual Encouragement and Empowerment: *What's in the Way IS the Way* by Mary O'Malley; Graham Cooke's "The Art of Thinking Brilliantly" YouTube Video Series; *Making of an Ordinary Saint* by Nathan Foster; and *Prayers From the Heart* by Richard Foster

For Complicated Breast Reconstruction: Northwestern Specialists in Plastic Surgery-Dr. Fine at www.nsps.com

Health information and Integrative Treatment: The Block Center for Integrative Cancer Care at www.blockmd.com

Other cancer stories: Jason Micheli at www.tamedcynic.com, Chris Wark at www.chrisbeatcancer.com

All-around good book: *Being Mortal* by Atul Gawande

Breast Cancer Info, Tips and Humor*: 100 Perks of Having Cancer plus 100 Health Tips for Surviving It*, Florence Strang, M.Ed. and Susan Gonzalez, B.S.N.

Non-traditional Cancer Survival and Prevention Information: www.Chrisbeatcancer.com; Veronique Desaulniers at www.breastcancerconqueror.com

Facts and Figures: The American Cancer Society at www.Cancer.org

Nutrition and Wellness Products/Research Updates: Dr. Mercola at www.mercola.com and Dr. Axe at www.draxe.com

Creative Expressions regarding Cancer: Twist out Cancer/Brushes with Cancer Event at www.twistoutcancer.org

Music: Yo-Yo Ma, Casting Crowns, Brooke Fasier, Hillsong Worship, Bethany Worship, Elevation Worship and many others with a positive message.

About the Author

Sarah Fenlon Falk is a smalltown girl from Cheboygan, Michigan who wanted to live in "the big city." She moved to Chicago, Illinois after achieving her Master's degree in Clinical Social Work from Michigan State University. She remained single much longer than she had anticipated or desired. Her husband, Pete, was very much worth the wait, she will tell you! Together they have four beautiful boys and a trained therapy dog named Molly.

Sarah has written all of her life, beginning her journaling legacy at the age of six. Just before being diagnosed with cancer for the second time in her life, Sarah decided it was time to write more seriously and consistently. She chose to document her journey through breast cancer in the hopes of encouraging and inspiring others. She is a public speaker and has shared her story at various speaking events in the Midwest and through her blog/website.

Finding Myself...Facing Cancer is her first book. Sarah plans to publish a non-fiction workbook, *Keeping It Together: A Patient's Companion Through Decision Making* this summer as well as *The Servant Prince,* a fiction work for young readers, in the fall.

Sarah shares thoughts on wellness and thriving in the midst of struggles on YouTube and Facebook. Search and follow her at: Sarah Fenlon Falk.

She continues to share her story and life lessons in whatever way she can in an effort to encourage and empower her listeners/readers. For contact information and to keep up-to-date on Sarah's books, videos, or to book or attend speaking engagements visit: www.SarahFenlonFalk.com.